Audacious GOALS Remarkable RESULTS

How an Explorer, an Engineer
and a Statesman shaped our
Modern World

Brad Borkan and David Hirzel

© Brad Borkan and David Hirzel 2021

Brad Borkan and David Hirzel have asserted their moral right
to be identified as the authors of this work in accordance
with UK and US copyright law.

All rights reserved.
Without limiting the rights under the copyright reserved above,
no part of this publication may be reproduced, stored in, or introduced
into a retrieval system, or transmitted, in any form, or by any means
(electronic, mechanical, photocopying, recording, or otherwise),
without the prior written permission of the authors.

ISBN 978-1-945312-14-4

Terra Nova Press
P. O. Box 1808
Pacifica CA 94044

Dedication

Brad Borkan:
To my daughter, Brittany Borkan,
I am so very proud of you. Continue to follow
your passion, and above all, dare greatly.

David Hirzel:
To my sister, Nancy Jeanne Hirzel, who knows me best
and longest, who has been by my side and encouraging
my writing as long as I have been at it. Your support and
confidence in me and my work has been one of the mainstays
of my life, and whatever success I may have had in it.

Contents

The NASA Mars Rover	8
Man In The Arena Speech	10
Prologue: It's Your Call	11
Introduction: Monumental Impact	14
Part One: Bold In His Plans: The Engineer	**24**
1 Undaunted by Challenge: The Tunnel That Changed Our Modern Cities	26
2 A Bottle Of Wine Set Aside	35
3 The Thames Tunnel's Immense Legacy	44
4 Thinking Audaciously: The Railway That Transformed How Time Is Measured	48
5 More Than A Set Of Tracks	58
6 The Great Western Railway's Dazzling Legacy	68
Part Two: Daring Greatly: The Statesman	**76**
7 Even A Bullet Couldn't Stop Him	78
8 Seizing Opportunities: The Origins Of The World's Conservation Movement	80
9 Preserving Nature And Wildlife On A Grand Scale	90
10 A Legacy Of Conservation	96
11 Solving the Right Problem: The Waterway That Accelerated Global Trade	104
12 Competing Visions For The Canal	114
13 The Monumental Legacy Of The Panama Canal	125
Part Three: Let No Obstacle Turn You Back: The Explorer	**132**
14 The Open Window	134
15 Adventure Is Just Bad Planning: The 500-Year Quest For The Northwest Passage	136
16 Planning To Succeed Where Others Had Failed	147

17	The Enduring Legacy Of Amundsen's Quest For The Northwest Passage	161
18	Synthesizing Everything You Have Learned: Reaching The Ends Of The Earth	166
19	False Starts, Crevasses And Letters To The King	174
20	The Legacy Of Achieving The South Pole	189

Part Four: Enduring Lessons — 192

21	Ten Lessons From An Explorer, An Engineer, And A Statesman	194
22	They Never Stopped Achieving	198
23	Movers And Shapers Of The Earth's Geography	215
24	The Greatest Lesson Of All	220
25	The Ultimate Legacy: Delivered In A Mars Rover Parachute	224

Appendix — 227

Timeline	228
Overlaps Of People And Project	236
Recommended Reading	237
Acknowledgements	245
Notes About The Photographs	248
About The Authors	249

For additional photographs and further information about this book, please visit our website: www.extreme-decisons.com

The NASA Mars Rover

On February 18, 2021, NASA's Rover spacecraft descended rapidly toward the planet Mars, after traveling over 290 *million* miles in just six months and twenty days. The event was broadcast live.

A smooth landing was crucial for the NASA Rover, and everything would come down to these critical final moments. A team of engineers had labored for eight years on this moment, but no amount of simulations on Earth could guarantee success landing in the rarefied Mars atmosphere.

One of the big unknowns was: would the red-and-white-striped parachute deploy at exactly the right time, and in the correct position, to slow the craft down? Failure would cause the spacecraft to crash onto the planet's surface, smashing this multi-billion-dollar project into fragments of twisted metal.

So what actually happened?

Everything worked perfectly. Exactly as planned.

The head of the NASA landing team, Allen Chen, announced the Rover's success at a press conference immediately after the landing. While explaining how they had achieved such a smooth touchdown, he also revealed that the arrangement of the parachute's red-and-white stripes might contain a coded message. This hint generated a lot of media interest, sparking an international race to decipher the message.

The Mars Rover program is modern proof of what happens when you combine **exploration**, **engineering**, and **political will** to achieve the seemingly impossible.

These three skills were central to the great endeavors described in the coming pages, all of which happened over a century before the Mars Rover landed, and helped shape the world we live in today.

In case you are wondering what the parachute's coded message said, all will be revealed *in the last chapter.*

"It is not the critic who counts; not the man who
points out how the strong man stumbles, or
where the doer of deeds could have done them better.

The credit belongs to the man who is actually
in the arena,

whose face is marred by dust and sweat
and blood; who strives valiantly; who errs,

who comes short again and again, because
there is no effort without error and shortcoming …

…and who at the worst, if he fails,

at least fails while daring greatly…"

—excerpt from "The Man in the Arena"
Theodore Roosevelt, April 1899

Prologue
It's Your Call

Imagine yourself, just twenty-one years old, in charge of one of the most talked about projects in the world: digging the first-ever tunnel beneath a free-flowing river. Not just any river, but one of the greatest rivers in the world, running through one of the most vibrant and populated cities in Europe.

This tunnel is a vast undertaking. It isn't just the length of the tunnel that is daunting, or that all previous attempts have failed. It is also the sheer magnitude of the project: the risk, danger, and hard work required to achieve something monumental.

The height and width of the tunnel is large, even by today's standards. Putting it in perspective, even with all our latest technology, the aperture would be greater in diameter than *almost every tunnel ever built*, including the Channel Tunnel connecting Britain to France.

Except the year is 1827, and this particular tunnel is being dug by hand, with pickaxes and shovels, through 1,200 feet of the shifting, treacherous, water-sodden sand, silt and gravel of the Thames riverbed in London. Nothing of this magnitude has ever been attempted before. The iron frame within which you and each of the workmen stand is based on a new, never-before-tested building technique. Success rests on your shoulders alone.

The world is watching, fascinated by the sheer scale and audacity of the project. If this tunnel is successful, it will prove the way for similar tunnels to be dug beneath rivers in the world's other great cities, ultimately improving trade, commerce, and the movement of people.

The exact thickness of the riverbed mud above your head is unknown, but it is not much, at times no more than a few feet at best. An accidental penetration into the river's channel will flood the tunnel in certain disaster. This is not clean, clear river water but Thames water, which for over 1,000 years has been the sewer of London, toxic beyond belief.

Already, seepage from above is responsible for the workmen's sickness, blindness, and is even causing death. You are in charge of the digging, and it is affecting your own health as well. The dangers are further compounded by the presence of many visitors paying admission to enter the recesses of the tunnel and watch the work.

Your greatest fear is that the tunnel face will edge too far into the thin layer of riverbed overhead and penetrate the channel above, and that an unstoppable flow of water will pour into the tunnel. If that happens everyone in it—tourists, your workmen, you—will perish. The greatest public works project of your era will, in a matter of minutes, come to a tragic, ignoble end.

On one evening, without the usual paying visitors in the tunnel, the first breach happens. Thames river water begins to drip, then flows—then surges full force—into the tunnel. Louder than a locomotive, the roar of it is literally deafening. You and the other workers run toward the open end of the tunnel leading to the riverside, desperately climbing the stairs there to safety. You follow them up, but stop.

This is *your* tunnel.

These are *your* workers.

One of the older workers who didn't make it to the staircase in time is thrashing about in the fast-rising water, struggling to keep his head above the flood. Ignoring your own instinct to save yourself, you grab a rope, slide down to the rising water on an iron pole, tie the rope around his waist, and hoist him up.

Remarkably, all of you survive the crisis. Will you be so lucky next time?

You know for certain there will be more breaches. The next one will happen when the tunnel is longer, when you and your workers will be even farther away from safety. The next breach will be deadly for certain.

Do you continue the work? It's your call.

This was a real event faced by a real twenty-one-year-old engineer. What he did next may surprise you.

Introduction

Monumental Impact

We all make decisions. It's a core element of being human.

But, how do we make **better** decisions?

One way we can is by looking at the big decisions made by people in history, and learning from what they did well, and where they faltered.

When we started writing this book, our aim was to inspire you with the true facts as to how eleven of the greatest undertakings in the past 200 years happened, and what large and small decisions drove those achievements.

Why eleven? Nine was too few, twelve too many. Ten read like a "top ten" list. Eleven felt about right.

Our challenge was simple: we wanted to explore the risky, dangerous and challenging decisions these visionary pioneers made while undertaking these eleven big endeavors. And we wanted to show people today the valuable lessons they can glean from these breathtaking, historical achievements—lessons that can be incorporated into everyday decision making.

That was our goal.

But, like many things in life, embarking on one path of discovery often leads to a place that is *startling, unexpected and exciting*.

Quite by accident, we noticed something odd about these eleven projects and the people involved in them. We narrowed our focus further, and eleven projects became six—this book reveals our shock discovery that forced us to change tack. What follows next is a series of surprising revelations about the six projects (the first of which you just started reading about—the Thames Tunnel) and the *three* remarkable people who made them happen.

But that's not all we discovered. These three great visionaries shared a set of traits that made them successful. Their personal stories are as risky as the projects that each strived valiantly to make a reality.

Just like we all do, they made good decisions and bad, incurred failures, and at times struggled mightily to the point of wondering if they should just give up, before finding a route through.

How eleven became six

To find our initial eleven achievements, we brainstormed a list of accomplishments with bold decisions attached. What circumstances led these people to get involved in these great endeavors, and to then see them through to completion? Who else was involved? What information did these people use in their decision-making process? How did they not give up at the first sign of failure?

The true-story achievements we searched for had to be bold undertakings, arising from the brilliant vision of one person or a team who then brought it to fruition.

But we were looking for more than that.

Put simply, the stories needed to astound readers with attention-grabbing elements that you would not expect. In one of our stories for example, the London-to-Bristol railway led to the synchronizing of time on a national level, which ultimately led to the creation of global time zones. Who could have imagined there would even be a connection between these two events? Many more legacies followed on from the railway line, and we are only scraping the surface by mentioning this one here.

We also wanted the eleven to be achievements that had withstood the test of time—at least half a century—and were so valuable to modern-day society it would be hard to imagine the world without them. We wanted physical, tangible entities still in existence today that can be visited by any adventurer wishing to experience these enduring outcomes of human ingenuity.

Then we added more criteria. These remarkable projects all had to have been achieved by equally remarkable people.

But we needed much more than a set of stories packed with historical dates and timelines. We needed to be intrigued by the exciting aspects of the tales, and the people who were actually there in the "arena" (as Theodore Roosevelt would have called it, in our opening quote of the book)—the people who directed the events and who made decisions in the heat of the moment—not only the good decisions that propelled the venture forward, but also the disastrous choices that led to catastrophe.

The visionaries behind the projects had to have faced:
- Go/no-go decisions,
- Life-and-death decisions, and
- Decisions fraught with risk and danger.

We sought out projects where the protagonists risked their careers, reputations and sometimes their lives to achieve them, where their personal involvement must have evoked a sense of moral poignancy within each of them. Did the risks to life and limb (their own and others) outweigh the ultimate gain the achievement would bring? And if so, how did they make this judgment?

Each of these projects must have required a combination of strong leadership, solid teamwork, endless resilience and hope for success against the odds. We scoured the achievements for inspiring lessons that could be applied to modern-day society—for men and women at any stage in their lives and careers, or for today's business and political leaders.

We added another layer to our demands. The endeavors must not only be improbable but so seemingly impossible that people would have exclaimed, "It can't be done." We asked ourselves, can we bring these projects of the past to life and start you, the reader, thinking about what you might have done if faced with similar decisions?

We debated back and forth about what achievements would go in the book. How far back in history, or how current would we venture? Were our time scales too restrictive? Would the invention of the internet feature in our process? What about the iPhone? What about the light bulb or the car, the building of the Golden Gate Bridge or the splitting of the atom? One could draw upon a variety of criteria.

Eventually, we identified eleven projects sure to thrill readers around the world.

1. **Building the first steam locomotive** that allowed people to travel faster than a horse could run.
2. **Building tunnels under rivers**, which transformed urban life.
3. **Laying the transatlantic cable**, enabling near-instant intercontinental communication.
4. **Establishing the US National Park system** that started land and wildlife conservation.
5. **Discovering the secret of manned flights** and the risks and dangers arising from the birth of aviation.
6. **Solving the centuries-long quest for the Northwest Passage**—a long-sought-after sea route connecting Europe to Asia via northern Canada.
7. **Creating the first internal combustion engine**, and the advent of motorized transportation—including cars, trucks and all-terrain vehicles.
8. **Building the Panama Canal** to connect the world's two largest oceans.
9. **Reaching the North and South Poles** and the mapping of the polar regions.

10. **Climbing to the summit of Mount Everest** and the triumph of individuals and teams conquering the "death zone" on the highest peaks on the planet.
11. **Exploring outer space** and early space travel.

We analyzed the list in different ways: by date; by decision criteria; by impact on the world then and now; by the people involved. We expanded on these areas and narrowed them to see what caught our interest.

No matter how much we reshaped the list, three individuals' names kept repeating across some of the eleven projects, revealing a surprising detail:

Across eleven of the greatest accomplishments that fit our criteria, three people were each involved in ...

not just one project that had a monumental impact on our world today, but *two*.

The three were: Isambard Kingdom Brunel, Theodore Roosevelt and Roald Amundsen. Brunel was instrumental in building the modern railway and the first tunnel under a free-flowing river (1820s and 1830s). Roosevelt was the driving force behind the building of the Panama Canal (begun in 1903) and expanding the National Park system (1901-1909). Amundsen was first to reach the South Pole (1911–1912) and was involved in the hunt for the Northwest Passage.

This raised many fascinating questions, for example, what was it about *these* three men that set them apart from others? How did they make their most important decisions? What can we learn from their experiences to help us improve our personal and business decision making?

We may not be building something as audacious as the Panama Canal, or digging through the silt under the River Thames to build a tunnel, or trekking across the frozen tundra to the South

Pole, but we all have dreams and goals. During the course of any week or a month, we each face challenges that could impact our ability to achieve our goals. As the stories unfold, we hope you gain inspiration and learn from what Brunel, Roosevelt and Amundsen did to overcome difficulties with far fewer resources than we have at our fingertips today.

What did these three people do differently to those who'd tried and failed before? What motivated them to ignore the naysayers, and to realize their vision, on not just one big endeavor, but *two* separate endeavors? How did they deal with ever-present risks and danger? They certainly were not perfect human beings, so how did they recover from embarrassing and high-profile failures connected to those projects?

As these questions became increasingly vital and fascinating, not just to us but to everyone we spoke to about our Eureka discovery, we promptly switched focus from the original eleven projects to the three individuals: Brunel, Roosevelt and Amundsen, and their *six* monumental endeavors.

The final six projects

As you will see in the chapters that follow, the ventures listed below are much more than their names imply. They are infinitely more than just a tunnel, a railway, a park, a canal, a sea voyage or a trek through the snow. They are moving testimonials to the nature of the human spirit, the need to achieve, and the desire to dream big to accomplish something both magnificent and lasting.

Isambard Kingdom Brunel:
- The Thames Tunnel
- The Great Western Railway

Theodore Roosevelt:
- The National Parks
- The Panama Canal

Roald Amundsen:
- The Northwest Passage
- The South Pole

This book will reveal the audacious goals that set these projects in motion, the incredibly hard work that went into achieving them (complete with all the setbacks along the way) and the remarkable results of each, including the legacy they left for our world today.

You will notice that these six ventures were land-and sea-based initiatives. They required the three leaders to conquer the Earth's terrain, while preserving its beauty and diversity. The projects also involved movement—getting from one place to another. At the very heart of these six undertakings is a common theme: the geographical diversity of our planet.

As for the people involved, not all were contemporaries of each other. Brunel died before either Roosevelt or Amundsen was born, but our research uncovered new and unexpected overlaps in their work, and the traits these three leaders shared. Amundsen and Roosevelt, in particular, had an opportunity to cross paths—a story you'll read about in Part Three.

Although each had different backgrounds, training, professions and passions—Brunel was an engineer, Roosevelt a statesman and Amundsen an explorer—there exists an unmistakable similarity in how they each viewed leadership, teamwork, risks and goals. This similar mindset can inform us as to how to adjust our own strategies when facing adversity, setbacks and failure. We might also learn how to stop for a moment and better celebrate our milestones and successes, and help build a sustainable world for future generations.

An age of achievement

These six projects, with three audacious leaders at the helm, helped to drive an age of achievement (roughly from 1825 - 1914) where an expansive scope of ideas shone a light on a future with unlimited possibilities.

The men's backgrounds couldn't have been more different. At one point Brunel's father ended up in debtor's prison in England. In contrast Roosevelt, who was a sickly child and bullied in school, was born into one of America's wealthiest families. Amundsen grew up at the time when Norway was pushing to gain independence from Sweden and establish itself as a proud country on the world stage. Brunel's Great Britain was at the height of its power, while Roosevelt's United States was just coming into its own. Regardless of background or nationality, each of these game-changing leaders demonstrated shared key motivators: the desire to think big, to act boldly, to learn from their mistakes in the unforgiving school of hard-knocks and to keep striving to achieve their goals.

Not much stopped them in their quest for success. Bullets, blizzards, fires, floods, frostbite, landslides, serious injuries, and thwarting adversaries and naysayers were all part of a day's work.

And all of them kept going, long after the six projects ended, to influence the direction of some of the other original eleven projects.

Inspiring lessons for modern life

Yet, central to all of this is the human-interest story: of people working with others, and sometimes failing, but always picking themselves up and trying again. The three men were certainly not perfect decision makers or perfect human beings, but time and again they strived against the odds to show that the impossible could be accomplished. They were individuals who proved that dreaming big and planning large, combined with hard work, can lead to remarkable results.

This lesson is as valid today as it was in the era that Brunel, Roosevelt and Amundsen lived in.

The big reveal

We introduce each man with a bang—in one case literally. We jump into the action of their six big projects, ending each section with the legacy the project passed down to us and how we can use the lessons from these endeavors to improve our own lives.

At the end of the book, we include a startling revelation—derived from years of researching, thinking and writing about these outsized enterprises—that will show how you can incorporate the Brunel-Roosevelt-Amundsen approach into your own projects and career, and how it might even provide a way to approach some of the big societal challenges of our day. And, we reveal what was written in code on the NASA Mars Rover parachute.

Now, let's get back to the first of these projects—the Thames Tunnel.

In our prologue, *It's Your Call*, we left the resilient, and uniquely named, Isambard Kingdom Brunel in the midst of a disaster: the first (but not the last) tunnel flood.

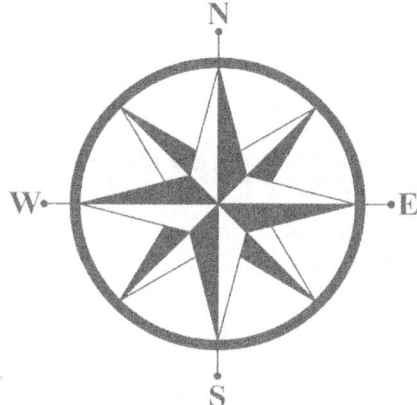

Part One

Bold In His Plans: Isambard Kingdom Brunel

The Engineer

"By his death the greatest of England's engineers was lost, the man with the greatest originality of thought and power of execution, bold in his plans, but right. The commercial world thought him extravagant, but although he was so, things are not done by those who sit down and count the cost of every thought and act."

—*Daniel Gooch, an engineer of the Victorian era, and a contemporary of Isambard Kingdom Brunel*

The Thames Tunnel as it appeared when it first opened.

Chapter 1
Undaunted by Challenge

The Tunnel That Changed Our Modern Cities

The breach occurred suddenly at high tide, on May 18, 1827. Thames River water rushed into the partially built tunnel. Isambard Kingdom Brunel (the twenty-one year old engineer on the project) and his men ran for safety to the shaft and climbed out using the ladders. Safely above the roaring water swiftly filling the chamber, Isambard heard one of the older workers cry out for help. Without hesitation or concern for his own safety, Isambard climbed down a metal rod and, using a rope, hauled the man out of the water.

All the men were saved. But what happened next is more interesting. Isambard hosted a banquet ... in the same tunnel.

Audacious, risky, remarkable?

Perhaps all three.

Welcome to the world of Isambard Kingdom Brunel, the engineer.

Tunnels

Try to imagine the urban world today without tunnels under rivers. We find them in cities everywhere, whether as part of our mass transit systems or the tunnels we drive through, connecting one shore to another. The island of Manhattan is connected to New Jersey via the Lincoln and Holland Tunnels. The United Kingdom is connected to France via a tunnel running beneath the English Channel. Tens of millions of people travel through tunnels every day while commuting for work, via the London Underground, the Paris, Saint Petersburg, Washington DC metros, California's BART and others. On mass transit systems, we pass through these tunnels barely noticing that we are even under water.

Yet, we probably never give much thought to how these tunnels came about, or that their existence followed on from the incredible story of the first tunnel built under a free-flowing river. The innovative engineering and the risks and dangers undertaken to achieve that *first* tunnel were immense, yet somehow this massive undertaking was accomplished. There are so many positive lessons we can learn from that build when thinking about adversity, challenge and dreaming big.

Two hundred years ago: why a tunnel was needed

Visitors to major European cities like London or Paris today can see the River Thames or the Seine from riverside esplanades, the water dotted with pleasure craft. In London you can travel from the city center to the popular Greenwich Royal Observatory by riverboat. In Paris, you can take an evening dinner cruise. The roads in these cities may be congested, but the rivers are fairly free of traffic.

Step back two hundred years, and you will see a different scene: a river clogged with boats piled high with cargo. Before the invention of cars, trucks and rail networks, most food and other merchandise arrived at their destinations on barges and ships. The riverside docks were congested with boats. Unloading them was a slow, labor-intensive process. The goods, once ashore, had to be moved by horse-drawn wagons through the town, by way of bridges over these rivers. Ships might have to wait at the wharf for several months to unload, putting their cargoes at risk of spoilage and theft.

More bridges to serve the growing urban populations were

desperately needed in the early 1800s, but river-based commerce serving a thriving city like London could not be halted by the disruption of building new bridges tall enough for ships to pass underneath. At the busy East London riverside docks, both the need and challenge were particularly apparent. Once a ship was unloaded, it was a long, slow traverse by horse and wagon to a bridge, where the goods would be moved across from one side of the river to the other.

It was clear—at least to some forward-thinking individuals—that a tunnel could be a solution, but there were overwhelming obstacles to the idea. No one in the world had ever built a tunnel beneath a flowing river. The Thames is a tidal river, its muddy bed partly visible at low tide. Ordinary tunneling through rock (mining) was well understood at the time, but tunneling through soggy, shifting material carrying the weight of a large river running over it presented an untried challenge.

Glorious failures

A tunneling project under the river involved digging vertical shafts on each opposing shore, down to the level where the horizontal tunneling could begin below water level, then excavating a horizontal shaft to connect them. The challenge, while easy to define on paper, was more difficult to solve in reality. The tunnel needed to be wide enough to accommodate the bi-directional movement of horse-drawn carriages. Each of the vertical shafts had to be wide enough to contain large circular ramps, enabling the horses and carriages to maneuver down to the tunnel level and back up to street level on the other side.

The very first tunneling attempt barely made any progress at all.

The engineer, Richard Dodd, designed the tunnel in 1799, but construction did not get very far before water began to flood the first shaft while it was being built. Wary investors halted the effort before any serious horizontal tunneling could begin.

A second attempt, eight years later, was designed and carried out by the renowned engineer Richard Trevithick. His plan was to build a pilot tunnel about the height and width of one man, which, once completed, would serve as a driftway to channel water seepage away from the construction of a much taller and wider tunnel excavated above it. He chose a location near Rotherhithe in East London where the Thames narrowed to a distance of 1,200 feet (365 m).

Trevithick's construction method, borrowed from standard mining procedures of the era, was simple: one man would dig at the face of the tunnel; another behind him would move the debris out of the way; a third man would shore up the newly exposed tunnel length with wood supports. Work on Trevithick's tunnel continued for over 400 days despite the incredibly cramped, hazardous conditions and the constant seepage of Thames water into the tunnel.

As tunneling neared the other shore, the tunnel flooded and the workers barely escaped with their lives. Realizing that the tunnel had hit a depression in the riverbed, Trevithick hired a boat to dump bags of clay onto the area above the breach. Surprisingly this worked, and the men were able to pump the tunnel dry.

Another breach resulted in a second disastrous flood. The money ran out, and the pilot tunnel was never completed, despite the workers achieving a remarkable distance of 1,000 feet (300 m) in length, eighty-five percent of the total distance needed. By the time work ceased, the remaining distance to the other shore was only about half a football field's length.

However, this was only the pilot tunnel. The rest of the project seemed an impossible task, and over fifty engineers of the era agreed: a tunnel large enough to handle commercial horse-drawn traffic could not be built under the Thames.

Needed: A completely different tunneling technique

Marc Brunel, father of Isambard Kingdom Brunel, had an impressive international career solving complex engineering problems.

An inspired inventor, the elder Brunel became intrigued by the challenge of building a tunnel under a river. He wanted to know: how do you bore a hole through riverbed silt and sand without it collapsing in on itself?

During a visit to a dockyard on the east coast of England, he picked up a discarded wooden plank belonging to the bottom of a ship under repair. Noticing it had several small holes, he took out a magnifying glass and studied it carefully.

He saw something fascinating.

The worm making the holes was using its jaws to bore through the wood. As it moved forward, it digested the wood and excreted a substance behind it that lined the hole, preventing collapse. This observation was the breakthrough Marc needed. The only question now was how to design a device that mimicked the worm's actions and was big enough to tunnel beneath a river.

Marc used this inspiration to create something that was both ingenious and unprecedented in design.

Wanting his only son to follow in his footsteps, Marc ensured the young man was well schooled in the fine art of engineering. By his late teens, Isambard Kingdom Brunel was already working in his father's design office, drafting working drawings for a suspension bridge and an innovative engine powered by carbon dioxide. By the age of nineteen, the young and fully trained engineer would be the first to put his father's invention, the Tunneling Shield, to full use.

A short, necessary description of Brunel's Tunneling Shield

This innovative device, patented in 1818, consisted of a series of cast iron frames or "cells." Each cell was both tall and wide enough for a single worker to stand in.

The cells were bolted together to form a "shield." The tunneling shield was a moveable framework, precisely the width and height of the tunnel bore itself. It was designed to sit at the face of the area being dug.

The cells were integral to the framework, set out in a pattern like identical-sized books on a group of shelves. One of the benefits of the design was that the cells could be stacked above and to the side, to achieve the desired height and width of the tunnel's aperture. For example, excavating a large tunnel might require 36 cells, set in 3 rows of 12 cells each, and a smaller tunnel might need only 15 cells, set in 3 rows of 5 cells each.

The cells enabled the men (all the tunnel workers at the time were men) to work in a coordinated, yet safe, manner, in complete isolation from each other.

How tunneling was achieved

In front of each worker within his cell were thick horizontal planks, each one the width of their cell, and approximately 8 inches (20 cm) tall. These boards formed a wall in front of the worker from the top of the cell to the bottom and held back the oozing mud of the tunnel face while the man worked.

A man standing within his cell and facing these horizontal boards could not see any earth to be dug at all, until he removed the screws holding the topmost board in place. After removing that one board, he would use a pickaxe and shovel to dig the earth revealed there, but only to a depth of about 4.5 inches (11.4 cm). When this bit of digging was completed, he would place the board back so it was flush against the earth, and tighten the screws to hold it in place.

The worker would then loosen the screws for the next board down, remove it and dig away another 4.5 inches, and screw it back into place, working his way down, one-by-one, to the lowest board. The men in each of the cells carried out this work simultaneously.

When all the boards within each cell of the cast iron frame had been shifted 4.5 inches forward, the *entire* Tunneling Shield was shifted forward that distance, and the tunnel would be 4.5 inches farther along than when the men had started.

Other men working behind them would constantly remove the water-laden soil being dug out, and another group of men would immediately brick up the area revealed by the forward movement

The Tunnel That Changed Our Modern Cities | 33

The Tunneling Shield in action (19th century lithograph).

of the frame, so the tunnel was simultaneously 4.5 inches longer and secure from collapse.

Why was distance of 4.5 inches chosen? Because it was approximately half the length of an ordinary London brick.

The only exposed tunnel face at any given time was one board width in each of the cells. There was always a risk of flooding while moving the frame forward, but with cement already mixed and everyone working in sync, the brickwork could be done quickly so that any breach of the 4.5 inch unsupported area—top, bottom or sides—would be minimized.

Brunel's Shield was only one of the essential ingredients in the overall work to achieve a tunnel.

The plan for the tunnel

Several years after the failure of Trevithick's tunnel, a few of its backers met to discuss the Tunneling Shield. Together, the backers formed the Thames Tunnel Company, appointing Marc Brunel as chief engineer.

His invention enabled the construction of a tunnel of virtually any dimension. The plan now was to build a tunnel that could enable bi-directional horse and carriage traffic. The tunnel would be:

- 35 feet wide and 20 feet high (10 m and 6 m).
- Starting at Rotherhithe and finishing at Wapping on the opposite riverbank.
- 1,200 feet long (365 m).
- And have only a very tight fourteen-foot margin (4.2 m) at its thinnest section below the River Thames.

All this would be dug as one big tunnel. Within it, a wall splitting the tunnel into north-and southbound carriageways would be constructed at the same time as the excavations. This wall would also strengthen the center of the tunnel.

But would it work?

The answer lay with the man who would dedicate himself to be on the scene, in the tunnel day after day, to make sure this totally new and untried scheme, with all its mechanical and human complexity, would succeed.

That person was Marc's son, Isambard Kingdom Brunel, who had only just graduated with a degree in engineering from a university in France.

Chapter 2

A Bottle Of Wine Set Aside

Marc Brunel's approach to digging the shafts from the riverbank down to the level of the tunnel entrance was strikingly different to those of Dodd and Trevithick. He calculated that to accommodate the movement of horse and carriages down a circular ramp, the shaft would need to be 50 feet in diameter and 50 feet deep (15 m).

Knowing that the riverside was relatively soft, Brunel planned to use this to his advantage. How? By building the entire structure of the brick shaft *above* the ground and letting it sink downward. Even today the idea sounds surreal: to dig 50 feet below ground you must first build 50 feet above ground!

The process would begin with the construction of an iron ring 50 feet in diameter that would sit on the riverbank. It would have a similar-sized circular brick wall built on top of it. Once the wall was fully completed *above ground*, the workmen would stand within the cylinder and dig out the soil directly below the iron ring. As earth was removed the structure would sink gradually into the ground, in a controlled manner.

Construction began in March 1825 with a ceremony attended by over 200 people. Marc Brunel placed the first brick on the iron ring, and nineteen-year-old Isambard placed the second. On that same day, a bottle of wine commemorating the occasion was set aside, to be opened at a future celebration dinner after the entire tunnel project was completed.

As we venture further into this father and son story, there must have been many moments during the construction when they wondered if they would ever open the bottle, or if they would still be alive to drink it. The dangers of digging under the Thames might well kill one or both of them.

Building the shaft above ground was relatively quick. Bricklayers were *each* adding 1,000 bricks per day to it. It soon became a high publicity project: royalty, dignitaries, politicians and others visited the site to watch the progress.

In six weeks, the above-ground ring of bricks was complete and estimated to weigh 1,000 tons (the equivalent of about 250 elephants). Nine weeks later, the shaft had been sunk to the desired depth and underpinning begun. The shaft still exists today, in the exact place where it had been sited.

Life-and-death risks

The iron Tunneling Shield, constructed at a foundry and delivered to the site in pieces, was installed at the bottom of the new vertical shaft. Horizontal digging began in November 1825.

Progress was slow. More seepage than expected occurred at the tunnel face, and with no driftway passage to remove the water, the workers at the lowest level of the Tunneling Shield were knee-deep in foul-smelling and potentially lethal Thames water. The water was so toxic it could render a man temporarily, or even permanently, blind.

John Armstrong was hired as the resident engineer, with Isambard serving as his assistant. Early into the tunneling process, Marc Brunel became seriously ill. Six months after tunneling started, Armstrong also became so ill he was forced to resign. Their ailments at the time were not thought to have been related to the tunnel.

Young Isambard was handed an extraordinary opportunity because of his father's position and the illnesses of the other engineers. In January 1827, the twenty year old found himself in charge of the biggest, most challenging engineering project in Europe, and quite possibly the world.

Isambard took his role seriously and led by example, at times spending as much as thirty-six straight hours in the tunnel, working and catnapping where possible. His father hired three assistant engineers to work with him, but within two months one had died after contracting a fever while working in the tunnel, and another lost his sight in one eye and never fully recovered. Today, health and safety concerns would have shut down operations permanently. Back then, work continued as usual.

To add to the drama, the directors of the Thames Tunnel Company were unhappy with the slow rate of progress, and insisted that the screws holding the horizontal boards be extended so that rather than digging 4.5 inches (11.4 cm) before moving the board forward, the men would dig 9 inches (almost 23 cm). Their new directive made the risk of a breach from the unsupported section a much greater likelihood.

Around the same time, the directors also discovered that the public would pay money to see the tunnel development underway, regardless of the dangers it posed to everyone involved. Despite protests by both Brunels, in early 1827 and with one quarter of the tunnel's length completed, the Tunnel Company advertised that people could pay a shilling (in today's money about 4 US dollars) to descend the shaft, and enter the horizontal tunnel to see the tunneling work in action. Seven hundred people flocked to visit the site each day.

It must have been a highly memorable, if dimly lit, event.

The tunnel work continued through the spring and summer, but the soil conditions were fast becoming precarious. Gravel was being dug through more frequently rather than the more stable clay materials previously encountered. With the tidal movement of the Thames shifting the riverbed above, and the doubling of the distance of the supporting screws, the dangers grew with every passing day.

The first tunnel flood

The tunnel flood described in the Prologue: *It's Your Call* was the first time the tunnel had been breached. Given the inherent danger of the project—the varying depth of the river and the relative thinness of the layer of mud above the tunnel ceiling, a breach was not entirely unexpected. But Isambard had no idea exactly what would happen should such a failure occur—a seepage? Part of the tunnel face sloughing off? A catastrophic deadly torrent?

When he later wrote about this event, Isambard didn't write from a sense of fear but from one of excitement, recalling the exhilaration he felt when the surge of water hit the tunnel, and its deafening roar that was louder than a cannon blast. The near lethal breach had opened his eyes to the challenges of floods, and he sought new ways to correct them.

The day after the flood, a boatman rowed Isambard out on the River Thames, above where the breach had happened. Using a diving bell, he descended into the murky river water to inspect the damage.

It was what he expected. The tunnel had hit a depression in the riverbed.

His solution was the same as Trevithick's: drop bags of clay into the water at the site of the breach until the hole was plugged and the water stopped flowing in.

It took months to secure the tunnel and pump out the foul-smelling water. With his father ill and unable to work, the direction of the tunnel work fell entirely on young Isambard's shoulders. He became the decision maker.

If *you* were in his shoes, what would *you* have done?

The tunnel had flooded once, and Isambard knew it would flood again. His men were dying from exposure to Thames water, and toxic fumes from the oil lamps were also adding to the lethal dangers. The farther the tunnel was driven the greater the risk from both hazards.

And, the farther along a breach occurred, the longer the race to safety.

To Isambard, this tunnel build was more than the simple creation of a passageway for horses and carts. It represented the emergence of London as an even greater hub of commerce, to be at the cutting-edge of a grand future for those who had the vision to see it. Instead of dwelling on the flood as a disaster, Isambard decided to throw a banquet for fifty dignitaries instead— in the same tunnel that had only just been cleared of mud and debris, had almost killed him and his men, and was still at grave risk of flooding again.

The banquet

Isambard oversaw all preparations to ensure the event, scheduled for November 10, 1827, was sufficiently elaborate:

- Red cloth was used to line the interior section of the tunnel where the main banquet was to be held.
- Beautiful chandeliers were installed and lit.
- To add pomp and flair, music was provided by the prestigious Band of the Coldstream Guards, the oldest regiment in the British Army.
- Long tables were covered in white linen and set with silver and crystal, all in preparation for the invited guests.

The banquet was a huge success. George Jones, the director of The Royal Academy of Arts in London, commemorated the event in a painting.

Eager to also recognize the efforts of his 120 workers and staff, Isambard arranged a second banquet on the same evening in a different part of the tunnel. As a gesture to show Isambard he was really one of them, the workers presented him with a pickaxe and shovel, and toasted "To our tools."

It seems remarkable, even in today's world, that anyone would have the audacity to turn a near disaster into a feast, at the very site where the narrowly-averted debacle had occurred. But this was not how Isambard saw the world. Instead to him:

- Discomfort and risk were likely a daily occurrence in the pursuit of noble goals,
- Danger and near death generated excitement, and
- Marketing, elegance and confidence of success were as essential to a project as the engineering.

And yet, at this point, Isambard was still a mere twenty-one years old!

Death visits the tunnel

Work continued on the tunnel throughout 1827 and into 1828, adding another 56 feet (17 m) to its length. It had almost reached the halfway point.

In early January 1828, Isambard was working down below when a problem developed at the tunneling shield. Two men were having difficulty fixing some shoring supports inside one of the cells of the shield. Isambard went to their aid. Just then, a torrent of river water rushed in, swamping the area and threatening to drown everyone in the shield, including the bricklayers and the men removing the dug-out debris. The surging water pushed Isambard along until a falling timber pinned him in place. He freed himself and called for the others to follow him as he ran for shelter into one of the middle archways in the dividing wall, between the north and southbound carriageways of the tunnel.

Trapped in the murky darkness (the floodwaters had extinguished all the kerosene lanterns), Isambard and his workers felt their way back to the tunnel entrance and tried to escape up the workers' staircase in the shaft. But when Isambard arrived at the stairs he found the way clogged with fleeing workers. Fearing for his life, he turned and ran for the visitors' staircase.

There, he discovered men scrambling up and out of the shaft as fast as they could. Before Isambard could do the same, the floodwaters rushed forward in one enormous wave, rapidly filling the vertical shaft. At the top, his assistant was working feverishly to haul men to safety.

Isambard was close to drowning.

A hand reached out for him suddenly and pulled him to safety. His assistant was surprised to find the man he had just rescued was Isambard.

But not everyone had been so lucky.

Four workers died in the wave as it hit the stairway, rose up, and just as quickly receded.

Isambard suffered internal injuries and had cut his leg badly, but that didn't stop him. Hobbling in pain around the site, he immediately gave orders to procure a diving bell to inspect the breach in the riverbed. Too injured to go into the diving bell himself, he lay down on the barge that floated the diving bell into the River Thames and directed diving operations from there. He refused to leave until a complete assessment of the damage was carried out.

Despite his dedication to the success of the tunnel, Isambard's injuries were so severe that he never worked inside it again. While recovering in Clifton, near Bristol, he discovered a new focus: to design elegant bridges and completely transform how railways worked *(described in the next chapter)*.

By the end of March 1828, the tunnel was secure. Under the guidance of the remaining engineers on the project, the water was drained out and the work resumed. Visitors once again thronged to the site to see the tunnel shield and observe the repair work.

But the company was running out of money fast.

Appeals to raise funds were unsuccessful, and the tunneling shield was bricked up in August 1828.

The Great Bore

While *The Times* of London mocked the tunnel, calling it "the Great

Bore,"[1] the public still wanted to descend into the tunnel. A clever illusion was created by installing a large mirror on the new brick wall in front of the Tunneling Shield, making the tunnel appear even longer than it was.

For the next six and a half years, the company sought funding to complete the tunnel, and no further construction was undertaken. It was not until 1835 that enough money was raised to resume work. The additional funds enabled safety improvements to be made, including a redesign of the tunnel shield to strengthen and widen it, to prevent further breaches.

The perseverance paid off, and in November 1841, almost sixteen years after horizontal tunneling had first begun, the tunnel reached the second shaft on the Wapping side of the River Thames.

In March 1843, the tunnel was finally completed.

What happened to the bottle of wine?

Precisely eighteen years and twenty-three days had elapsed since that first day the bottle of wine was set aside to mark the occasion of the laying of the first bricks on the Rotherhithe shaft, to the official opening of the Thames Tunnel on March 25, 1843. Its first visitors were the paying public who walked the length of the tunnel in perfect comfort, from one side of the Thames to the other. It became known to many as "the eighth wonder of the world."

Marc and Isambard Brunel had achieved what fifty of their engineering peers told them was impossible: building a tunnel under the River Thames large enough to accommodate a horse and carriage. (In fact, their tunnel enabled horse-and-carriage traffic to travel in both directions simultaneously.)

On the first day, over 50,000 people walked through it. Over the next fifteen weeks, more than one million people walked beneath the Thames. To put this in perspective, the entire population of London at the time was about two million people.

The appeal was greater than simply walking from one side of the river to the other. The tunnel also became the first underground shopping arcade, complete with entertainers and food vendors.

Years later, long after the Brunels had ceased their involvement in the project, the activities of the vendors controlling tunnel trade turned seedy, and this engineering marvel became overrun with prostitutes and petty criminals. The tunnel was sold in 1869 to a public transit network that would later become the London Underground.

It is still in use today.

Chapter 3

The Thames Tunnel's Immense Legacy

The legacy of the Thames Tunnel is enormous.

The Tunneling Shield, which had its first-ever use in the construction of the Thames Tunnel, has been central to the creation of *every* bored tunnel since then.

One of the most famous bored tunnels to use this approach is the Channel Tunnel on the train route from Paris to London. That tunnel is over 31 miles long (50 km).

The bored-hole aperture, or opening, of the Thames Tunnel has a height of 23 feet and width of 37 feet (7 m by 11 m). This makes it one of the top ten largest bored-hole tunnels in the world. None of the tunnels of the Channel Tunnel are as wide as this, and Brunel's Thames Tunnel was entirely dug out with shovels and pickaxes. The Channel Tunnel and all modern tunnels were cut with large mechanical diggers.

As part of the London Underground rail network, the Thames Tunnel has been used continuously for train travel beneath the river for over 150 years.

Trains run through the tunnel daily at a rate of about one train every five minutes. Over fourteen million people use the train line each year. It is both the longest tunnel in the London Underground network and, surprisingly—given its age and the fact it has had very little work done to it since its completion—it is the one with the fewest leaks!

Its biggest legacy, however, is this:

> **The success of the Thames Tunnel helped to transform urban life in every river-straddling city in the world.**

With tangible proof that the tunneling shield technology worked, every city that straddled a river, including Paris, Frankfurt, Budapest and Vienna, now had a means to create a tunnel under their rivers. By coupling this urban innovation with train travel (in the next chapter, this is something else that Isambard Kingdom Brunel transformed) people no longer needed to live within walking distance of work.

This reduced the need for the densely packed tenement housing of the 1800s, and enabled cities to expand. These intertwined innovations triggered the start of suburban living, and reduced the need for multiple low-income families to live in the squalor of single apartments, in center city areas.

From the outset, the Thames Tunnel was much more than a tunnel. It was a pioneering innovation that not only transformed the world of the 1800s, but influenced the way we travel today. We think nothing of taking a subway or train that travels beneath a river, or driving through a tunnel beneath a river or a bay. These are now a commonplace occurrence—made possible by the success of the Thames Tunnel.

What is to be learned from the Thames Tunnel project that we can bring into our modern lives

- **Passion and perseverance—an unbeatable combination.** Marc and Isambard Brunel never lost their vision for the project, and persevered through almost impossible obstacles to make the tunnel a reality. Passion and perseverance underpinned their 'never give up on what you believe in' attitude.

- **Temporary physical discomfort may be part of the process.** By keeping his eyes firmly on the goal and understanding what benefits others would gain from his achievements, Isambard was able to tolerate the considerable discomforts of working on-site.

While most endeavors don't require digging through silt, sand and mud, every meaningful venture requires some element of discomfort and pain. The key to muddling through these tough times is achieved by accepting that short-term discomfort (for example, conquering a fear of public speaking) is a necessary part of achieving any great result.

- **Courageous decisions lead to better outcomes.** Isambard chose acts of courage over expediency or simplicity—whether it was rescuing a drowning man or facing the same daily risks his workers did. As shown in the other stories in this book, success and courageous choices often go hand in hand.

- **Some solutions might be found by observing the natural world.** Two great examples of this emerged from our tale. First, the tunneling shield design came from Marc Brunel's observation of how a woodworm made holes in a plank of wood. Second, assessing the soft soil on the banks of the River Thames gave birth to the brilliant idea of building the shaft above ground and sinking it. Inspiration for projects, big or small, can come from the physical world around us, and other unexpected sources.

- **When everything fails and disaster strikes, plan a banquet.** Isambard didn't hide disaster, he celebrated it. Staging your own grand public gesture, small intimate gathering, or even opening a bottle of champagne after reaching a milestone or recovering from a disaster, can rejuvenate your team.

How to experience the Thames Tunnel today

The Thames Tunnel is easy to visit if you are in London, and you can even travel through it. On the site of the Rotherhithe shaft (the shaft built above ground that was eventually sunk into the soft riverbank) is the Brunel Museum. The museum houses a wonderful collection of artefacts and details on the tunnel's construction. As part of the museum tour, you can descend into the shaft only. There is no longer any pedestrian access through the tunnel—it is today far more useful to the hundreds of London Underground trains that pass beneath the river every day.

You can travel through the Thames Tunnel by taking a train from the new Rotherhithe station (a short distance away from the museum) to Wapping station, one train stop away. Alighting at Wapping station enables you to look back inside the tunnel and see its original brickwork. Each and every brick that is visible in the tunnel was placed there by Brunel's workers. It must have been a momentous occasion when those last bricks were laid and the tunnel was finally connected to the Wapping shaft.

The Tunneling Shield no longer exists. Marc Brunel fought for its preservation, but it had to be scrapped to help recover costs after the project finished. Thankfully, the George Jones painting of the banquet still exists, and can be viewed at the Brunel Museum.

Fate has a way of interrupting even the best-laid plans. Still a young man when he was seriously injured in the second tunnel flood, Isambard left London and the tunnel project behind, to begin his recuperation. Had he not been injured he probably would have spent several more years working in the tunnel, and his future career would have become more intertwined with his father's.

While on bed rest in another part of the country, Isambard launched his career in a completely different direction. The next project he worked on—the London-to-Bristol Great Western Railway—had an even greater impact on the world. And this one he did without his father.

Isambard's vision for his new project? A railway, but one that was a whole lot more than tracks and trains.

> "... the railway is in progress. I am their engineer to the finest work in England."
>
> —*Isambard Kingdom Brunel's diary at the end of 1835*

Paddington Station as it appears today.

Chapter 4
Thinking Audaciously

The Railway that Transformed How Time is Measured

Bold new ideas are often brought to market by youthful vigor and imagination. Computer technology in the 1980s was driven by Steve Jobs and Bill Gates, when they were both under 30 years old. In a similar way, the railroads and railway technology, first developed in the 1830s, arrived in leaps and bounds because of efforts by Isambard Kingdom Brunel (aged twenty-five), Robert Stephenson (aged twenty-six) and Daniel Gooch (aged twenty-one).

But it was Isambard Kingdom Brunel who had the greatest, most lasting effect on railroad design as we know it today.

Just as Steve Jobs had a *vision* for the power of computers, exemplified by the first Macintosh, Brunel had a *vision* for railways. Brunel's grand idea for the London-to-Bristol train line changed the way the industry approached design because Isambard had the skill and temperament to make his vision a reality. And like Steve Jobs he persisted, despite high profile setbacks and failures along the way.

Brunel's plan for the Great Western Railway became the template for every train journey undertaken today anywhere in the world. His London-to-Bristol line, including the stations, bridges and viaducts, and the journey it takes across Britain, remains to this day largely as Brunel designed it.

This is its story and its legacy, including how this particular railway helped to influence two other important human achievements: the start of electronic communication and creating a better measurement of time.

The evolution of an idea

The earliest railway cars carried coal, not passengers. Pre-industrial Britain had long burned coal for heating, and British miners had learned from experience that carts with wheels rolling on wooden or iron rails, known as waggonways, moved heavier loads of coal with less effort than on paths made of earth. These mining tracks became the first 'railways,' but the first carts were pulled along by either men or horses.

Steam power had been in use since at least 1698, running the pumps that kept the subterranean mining tunnels dry, and powering stationary hoists to winch the raw material out of the ground. But never had it been used to move goods along tracks—until one person envisioned how to do this over a century later.

Richard Trevithick (the man introduced in the previous chapter who attempted unsuccessfully to build a tunnel under the River Thames) conceived the idea that wheeled carts and steam powered engines could be combined to improve how coal was transported. In 1802, at the age of thirty-one, he designed and built the first steam locomotive. His use of this machine to pull coal-filled carriages in the mines was successful, but it was still considered a novelty idea.

It was almost a quarter century later that passengers first traveled on above-ground railway tracks initially designed for moving coal from the northern England collieries of Darlington to the River Tees in Stockton. The locomotive engine was built by the father-and-son engineering team, George and Robert Stephenson. The first train journey had a mix of carriages for coal and flour, with a separate carriage for eighteen passengers, shaped like a stagecoach carriage. People were keen to experience this new form of transport, and the journey proved that railroads could move both cargo and paying customers. The idea of interurban passenger service was about to be born.

In 1830, Robert Stephenson's steam engine locomotive called the *Rocket* was the first intentionally designed to pull passenger carriages. Despite its name, the *Rocket* only averaged speed 12 miles per hour (19 km/h), with a top speed of 30 miles per hour (48 km/h). Slow by today's standards perhaps, but it is worth considering that from the time humans first appeared on Earth until this point, unless you were on the fastest horse or literally falling off a high cliff, very few if any humans would have traveled at 30 mph and certainly not over sustained distances.[2]

This idea that trains could be run overland to connect cities was already in effect by 1831, when Brunel took his first journey on the still-primitive railway line between Manchester and Liverpool. This bumpy, jarring, unpleasant ride convinced him that although the idea of intercity railway travel was sound, the haphazard execution he just experienced was not. Brunel found the travel slow, the tracks uneven, and the ride a torturous jostling from the first stop to the last. Railroads at the time had been conceived and designed to move goods, and while cargo could stand a bit of jostling, paying passengers would not.

Brunel, who could draw a perfect circle freehand (a skill he learned as a young boy), tried to draw one while riding on the train. The very imperfect, wobbly circle still exists in the Brunel archives. "The time is not far off when we shall be able to take our coffee and write while going noiselessly and smoothly at 45 mph," he wrote that night. "Let me try."

A ribbon of iron rails

Isambard Kingdom Brunel did not invent the railway, but his creative mind and engineering ingenuity enabled him to imagine a much-improved one. He first worked on a railway line project connecting one city to another. Later on, he envisioned a vast, regional network of level and well-laid tracks that would transform the humble mining cart into the fast, efficient rail travel we see today.

Brunel's grand idea was not all altruistic. He saw the immense profit that could be realized by those who understood and invested, not only in the mercantile trade between cities, but in the transportation upon which that commerce would quickly come to depend. The very idea of a rail connection enabling the fast movement of people and goods, and tying cities—even nations—together, would make forward-thinking investors fabulously wealthy.

But Isambard Brunel was not driven as much by wealth, as he was by ideas. The railway he envisioned could not exist until the right individual, with the right background to comprehend the vast possibilities, became involved. Someone who could combine these ideas to create a comprehensive framework that would link the world through a transportation network, forever changing the way we live, trade and work.

Brunel was that individual.

It is this idea for which we owe him so much. Had it not been for his vision and his unbridled ambition, and his energy and ability to overcome setbacks, these feats of railroad engineering would have taken much longer to be realized, in much different forms. The history of industrial development might have unfolded in a very different way.

Taking advantage of every opportunity

After the second Thames Tunnel flood severely injured him, twenty-three year old Brunel spent the bulk of his recuperation time in Clifton, an affluent part of Bristol, a growing city on the west coast of England. Not one to sit idle, Brunel became involved in numerous projects around Britain: experimenting with engines powered by gas pressure rather than steam, designing drainage ways and docks, and surveying bridges and canals.

One of the projects that intrigued him was a competition to design a bridge over the Avon Gorge, a picturesque area near Bristol. Brunel's convalescence had given him plenty of time to consider the aesthetics of a bridge set high above the Avon River, as well as the structural requirements that would ensure its long-term viability. Brunel boldly submitted four plans, each one set in a different location along the river. These architectural drawings, along with separate plans he created for repairing the Bristol Docks, caught the attention of Bristol city leaders, and ultimately led to a meeting with a committee of investors interested in connecting their growing city with London.

When the committee of what was then called the Bristol and London Railroad appointed Brunel as chief engineer, they set him a huge challenge: design and build the entire Bristol-to-London train line. At that point in time, if successfully completed, it would be the longest railway line in the world.

Brunel had both the education and creative energy to dream big and to execute his ideas. What he lacked was any real experience in building a railway. But in those early days of rail, few, if any, engineers knew anything about building a railway, let alone across such a distance as was being proposed.

Brunel brought with him a wealth of new ideas and engineering solutions to the table to address the myriad of logistical problems inherent in pre-Victorian transportation. What became the greatest transportation system Victorian England had ever seen, provided the world with the blueprint for further railway development. And it all came from Isambard Kingdom Brunel's fertile imagination and doggedly analytical mindset.

A canal system for moving heavy goods already existed; the only interurban railway in all of England connected just two cities, Liverpool and Manchester—and not very efficiently. Bold, new designs were needed to make better use of stone, brick and cast iron to construct new bridges, viaducts and trestles. These were especially important because Britain was heavily intersected by rivers, streams, marshes, valleys, and the occasional gorge. Mining techniques of the day had to be adapted to tunnel, or cut, through any hill standing in the way of a level path. New designs for the boilers and pistons of steam-powered locomotives were needed to develop the power and speed to make this a fast and highly efficient transit system. Each new idea led to another, building on successes and abandoning failures along the way.

Brunel shared three compelling traits with Roald Amundsen and Theodore Roosevelt, the other two subjects of this book. What they all had in combination was: the desire to learn from every experience; the training, inspiration and ambition to refine technologies that already existed; and the ingenuity to harness these refinements while recognizing that failures will certainly happen along the way.

The engineer

When Isambard Kingdom Brunel was named the Company's Engineer (what would now be called the Chief Engineer) for the Great Western Railway, the enterprise had no train carriages, no engines to pull them, and no tracks to guide them. The position had been created by a committee, and intended in the larger, contemporary sense: "a person skilled in mathematics and mechanics, employed in delineating plans and superintending the construction of public works, as aqueducts and canals."[3] For the newly unfolding art of railway engineering design, this could have been extended to include "and railways with their routes surveyed to astonishingly precise gradients over the course of many miles, and the tunnels and bridges necessary to keep those gradients precise."

With all this in mind, no better man could have filled the position.

Bristol and London are separated by a distance of 116 miles (186 km). At the time, the terrain between them was crisscrossed by numerous rivers requiring bridges, hills to be tunneled through, and marshlands to go over or around. Brunel managed them all with the mathematical precision needed to create the most level route possible.

Brunel's goal was that ascents or descents never exceed 8 feet (2.4 m) in the course of 1 mile (1.6 km), reasoning that the more level the route, the faster the train could travel. He also kept to the traditional railway constraints that tracks could only accommodate sweeping bends rather than tight turns, when avoiding geological obstacles.

Brunel's devotion to such precision, especially when constrained by the relatively simple surveying instruments available to him in the early 1830s, cannot be overestimated. His journals are filled with details of locating the route, meandering as it does through the countryside, and describes his negotiations with wealthy landowners, and in some cases impoverished villagers, to secure the most level rights of way through their lands.

Working twenty hours a day

Brunel completed his exhaustive land survey in ten weeks. To achieve this he worked twenty hours a day, spending much of it riding on horseback for an average of 40 miles (65 km) per day. It was a remarkable achievement and a feat of endurance, when you consider the variety and topological complexity of the British countryside, as well as its temperamental climate.

At the start, Brunel worked with a small team all riding on horseback, but this method was onerous, as it required traveling back and forth to file reports. To do his part more efficiently, Brunel designed and commissioned a horse-drawn carriage survey office, naming it *The Flying Hearse*, complete with a compact sleeping area for his catnaps each night. This kept him in the thick of the work without interruption, and in the best position to lead his team from the front.

Wherever the prospective near level track bed had to cross a river, he imagined and then designed a bridge. The challenge with any train line approaching a river is that, given the path of the tracks mandated by the surrounding terrain, the train line may not come to a crossing at the narrowest point of the river.

Brunel had to constantly balance the route of the track with the varying width of the river, as well as deal with the challenge of

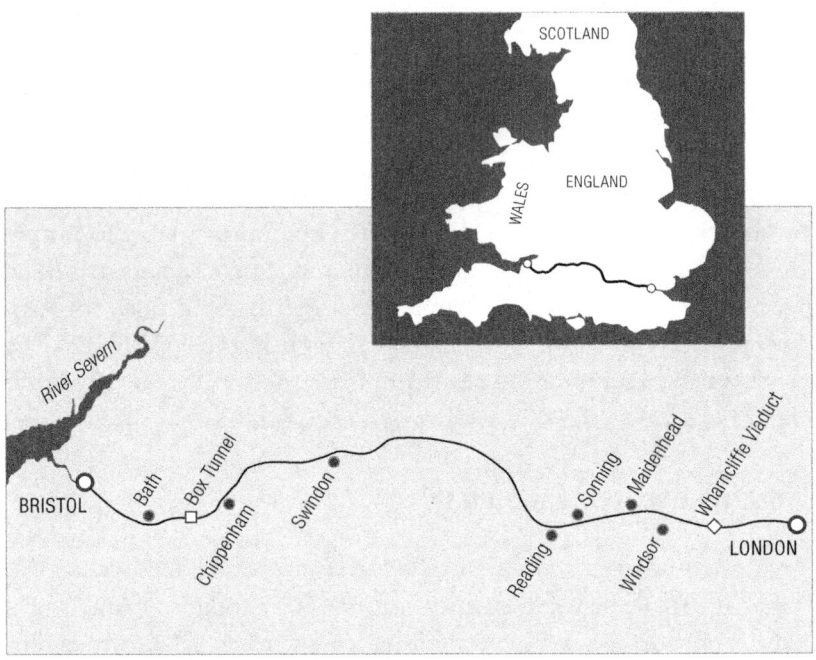

Route of the Grand Western Railway and key locations along the railway line.

creating a bridge high enough to allow boat traffic underneath, all while keeping within the very strict gradients that a train can traverse up and down. Even with all these constraints, Brunel not only managed to meet the demands but he designed supremely elegant structures—the majority of which are not only still standing today, but in constant use as well. (Of the few structures that were replaced, none were due to poor design or construction. It was due to additional tracks being required to meet modern consumer demand.)

Where his track encountered a very significant hill between Bath and Chippenham, Brunel imagined and then engineered the mechanics of how to bore the longest tunnel yet devised anywhere in the world—a two-mile-long tunnel (3.2 km) through the hard rock of Box Hill. Remember, the year was still 1835. Creating a tunnel of this size was an unimaginably difficult, well-nigh impossible project to carry off. (Brunel would know this only too well. When he started on this project, his Thames Tunnel was still stalled due to lack of funds. That Tunnel, which had been started years before, would not be finished until 1843, and it was only one-ninth the length of what he was proposing for Box Hill.) Brunel persevered through this and every other obstacle, and under his leadership the entire railway line was built. But it wouldn't have been successful had he not led from the front to make the impossible come to pass.

He did all this to achieve the most level route between London and Bristol.

Why Bristol?

The only hint we'll give you now is that it was the nearest port to the Irish Sea.

Chapter 5

More Than A Set Of Tracks

Brunel's vision for the London-to-Bristol line differed from the most commonly held views about railway lines. His focus was not simply to create a meandering path across the countryside, with stations and stop-off points at cities and towns.

His futuristic concept involved creating *a main trunk line* that would enable passengers to travel from one major city to another as quickly, efficiently and comfortably as possible, with only a small number of stops at key towns along the way. If passengers wanted to reach a town not on the main line, they would change to *branch lines* at designated interchange stations.

His idea flew in the face of an immense political challenge.

Windsor Castle—a royal residence—sits between London and Bristol, but not on the most level or direct path. Incorporating Windsor as a stop would have lengthened the route and slowed the train's journey time to Bristol by a considerable amount. Brunel reasoned that a far more efficient approach was to build a station at Slough or Maidenhead, both were on the more level and direct path of London to Bristol, and at one of these stations a passenger could change to another train for Windsor.

Another of Brunel's grand concepts was to design imposing,

beautiful structures as the London and Bristol terminus stations. Prior to this, a station might be a simple shed with a newspaper vendor.

To facilitate greater passenger comfort, he needed to make his stations grander and better equipped than previous railway facilities. He wanted horse-drawn taxi carriages to be able to pull up inside the station, so that passengers could go from the train right into a waiting taxi without getting wet. With his combined ideas the entire journey, literally from door-to-door, would be a memorable experience.

Brunel was more than just a skilled designer and visionary. He also had a wealth of political skills. Deftly defending the cost, construction and chosen route of the railway to the Houses of Parliament, he easily handled eleven days of cross-examination by politicians from all the political parties. Knowing every detail intimately, he patiently answered all questions thrown at him. He succeeded against formidable opposition from canal operators, stagecoach companies, landowners, and other railway builders who did not want any competition at all from these upstart railways.

In the end, Brunel's version of the line and its commerce-driven endpoints—envisioned to be destinations in and of themselves—prevailed.

Accepting failure

Isambard Brunel was not just focused on the broader issues of the route: the rail-line's overall structure and the design of its stations. He wanted to redesign everything about trains and train travel, and refused to take any detail for granted. (An analogy could be made to Steve Jobs' approach when he designed the first iPhone since that was a radical departure from any cellphone previously on the market.) For the railway, Brunel reassessed how train tracks could be designed, what materials might be used for the track bed and how it would be laid out, the locomotive's wheel and engine sizes, the passenger carriages and, most importantly, the gauge or width of the train tracks.

Brunel's designs and tests proved that a wider gauge (at 7 feet, or 2.1 m) would provide a more stable ride. Trains could have a lower center of gravity, making them both less prone to rocking and capable of travel at higher speeds. Wider trains would allow stronger locomotives to be used, and larger carriages would mean more paying passengers on each train, thus helping to recoup construction costs faster.

However, not all of his ideas were astounding successes.

Some were outright failures.

His early designs for rails, track beds, small-bore short-stroke steam pistons and vacuum-powered locomotives all produced dismal and embarrassing results. But failure did not daunt Brunel's spirit and enthusiasm for any project. To the contrary, his defeats only spurred him on to try harder, or find another solution—or both.

The early and mid-1830s was a time of progress. Rapid expansion of the train track network across northern Britain had begun, built to accommodate engines and passenger carriages already working at the smaller 4 foot 8½ inch (1.4 m) standard gauge. Although Brunel fought admirably to compel all train companies to change to his wider tracks (arguing it would be better for passengers), his efforts ultimately came to nothing.

Though his wider gauge was adopted by the Great Western Railway system, in the end the narrower gauge became the standard in use throughout the world. All the wider-gauge tracks used in the Great Western Railway had to be rebuilt to the narrower gauge years later because of a parliamentary commission ruling in 1846 that decreed the narrow measurement would become the standard track gauge for Great Britain. (Ironically, the 4 foot 8½ inch gauge was based on locomotives designed for use in narrow mines to carry coal, not people.)

Multi-tasking

To enable the Great Western Railway to enjoy some initial financial success, Brunel planned for the train line to be built in unconnected sections at each end of the route, before completing the middle section which required more complex engineering structures.

As soon as the track was completed on the eastern portion, the trains would start running from London to Reading, which was 34 miles (55 km) to the west. Similarly, once construction was completed on the far western Bristol-to-Bath section, service could begin between those cities. The aim was to sell tickets on the completed parts, to acclimate passengers to rail service. It would take Brunel and the Great Western Railway company a few more years before the middle Bath-to-Reading section would be finished, thus completing the London-to-Bristol service.

Remarkably, the Great Western Railway was not the only complex engineering project Brunel was working on at the same time. He was working at a frantic pace. During a quiet moment at the end of 1835, twenty-nine-year-old Isambard was sitting by the fireside when he composed a list of his accomplishments thus far. *"Clifton Bridge—my first child, my darling ... Sunderland Docks too is going on well ... Bristol Docks. All Bristol is alive and turned bold and speculative ... Merthyr & Cardiff Railway, Cheltenham Railway, Bristol & Exeter Railway ... Suspension Bridge across Thames—I have condescended to be engineer to this."*[4]

Having chosen every inch of the Great Western Railway route himself, Brunel knew each mile along the London-to-Bristol line intimately. He had personally designed the stations, bridges, the cuttings through hills, the embankments, the viaducts, trestles and tunnels. His assistants may have checked and rechecked his measurements, but Brunel was the designer and decision maker. Since many of Brunel's ideas pushed the boundaries of what was thought to be possible for an engineering work, he ended up designing the construction methods as well.

Failure, redesign and testing

Along the way there were many challenges to overcome. The location of the London station was one of them. Ultimately,

Brunel and the Great Western Railway were able to site a station at Paddington, in West London. In June 1838, with a temporary station in place, the first trains ran as far as Taplow, just outside of Maidenhead, over 20 miles (32 km) away.

The journeys were a disaster.

Not in the sense of a train crash thankfully, but in the quality of the ride and the power of the locomotives built to Brunel's specifications. His *Vulcan* and *Premier* locomotives had a number of flaws that were a direct result of his innovative, but badly engineered designs. In fact, the initial Great Western Railway service was so bone-rattling, it bore more than a resemblance to the Manchester-to-Liverpool ride that Brunel had derided years before. As a result, Brunel was very nearly fired by the Board of Directors.

Fortunately, Brunel had Daniel Gooch, a locomotive design engineer, on his team. Gooch was only 21 years old and had previous experience working for Robert Stephenson, the man who built the *Rocket* locomotive. Gooch solved the problems with Brunel's locomotives, enabling them to deliver more speed for less power. Gooch's connections to Robert Stephenson allowed the Great Western Railway to aquire two new locomotives from Stephenson's workshop called the *North Star* and *Morning Star*. Brunel insisted on overseeing the transfer of the *North Star* from a barge to the railway. Quick reflexes enabled him to escape death when the lifting tackle broke—just another day at the "office" for the intrepid engineer.

Gooch went on to design other locomotives used on the line. They had intriguing names like *Firefly* and *Lord of the Isles*. (Daniel Gooch will resurface on an altogether different project in a later chapter.)

The other major problem Brunel had was his track design. Stephenson liked to build his tracks as rigid iron rails fixed to stone blocks. Brunel preferred to attach his rails longitudinally to timber beams (called sleepers) that would be pinned at intervals with wooden stakes. But what these friends—and competitors—realized was that rigid tracks made for a rough ride. They both discovered that by not pinning the sleepers so tightly the rails had more give, resulting in a more pleasant journey for passengers.

Brunel viewed engineering challenges in seven dimensions

Similar to his days working on the Thames Tunnel and his time surveying the London-to-Bristol route, Isambard Kingdom Brunel worked long hours during the line build. He continued to routinely log up to twenty hours per day, shuttling between the London-to-Taplow line and the recently completed Bristol-to-Bath line. All that remained was to connect Taplow to Bath, but three significant challenges lay between the two ends: crossing the River Thames in the east part of Maidenhead, the hill at Sonning, and further west a lengthy, tall hill near the large village of Box.

A construction project like a bridge or a tunnel requires attention to three dimensions: height, length, and width. But Brunel's matrix had four additional components. Three of these were: how quickly the structure could be built, how long it would endure, and how soon it would generate revenue. As to the last consideration, Brunel had to focus on how fast the service could be brought into operation and begin generating funds to pay off the company's construction debt, and start generating a profit for the shareholders, to ensure their enthusiasm for future projects.

Having watched his father, Marc Brunel, suffer through various business venture setbacks, including the indignity of ending up in debtors' prison, the younger Brunel understood the importance of conquering funding issues head on. And for a man of Isambard's sensibilities, there was one more dimension, learned as a teenage apprentice to the world-renowned watchmaker Abraham Louis Breguet in Paris.

Beauty and function combined

The final element in Brunel's matrix was elegance.

Where Isambard Kingdom Brunel stood head and shoulders

above his engineering contemporaries was in his keen eye for design. He sought timeless, elegant designs that would stand up to the rigor of changing aesthetics. It is from this perspective that we now look at some of the major structures he designed for the London-to-Bristol railway.

Paddington Station, London: Paddington Station started out as a temporary structure. In the late 1840s, after the Great Western Railway had been running for years, money was finally found to construct an appropriate, permanent terminus. Brunel designed a glass-and-steel roofed structure that appears as modern today as it must have been when it was finally opened in 1854. At the time, the structure sported the largest train station roof ever built in the world.

Wharncliffe Viaduct, Hanwell: Ten miles (16 km) west of Paddington, Brunel faced his first major obstacle in the terrain: the marshland of the Brent Valley, too soft to carry train tracks and too wide to go around. So Brunel designed and built the magnificent Wharncliffe Viaduct: eight massive, yet elegant, brick archways supporting the train tracks above the marshland. It remains timelessly beautiful and is so strong that trains today run every few minutes across its length. It is the largest brick structure on the Great Western Railway route.

The viaduct ended up being more than just a set of arches. Brunel persuaded the board of the Great Western Railway to allow wires to be attached along the Wharncliffe Viaduct to facilitate the installation of a new electric telegraph system between London's Paddington station and a station west of Hanwell. This became the first ever installation of a commercial electric telegraph.

Maidenhead Bridge: Seventeen miles (27 km) west of the viaduct, the train line needed to cross the River Thames. At this location the river was quite wide. The challenge that Brunel needed to overcome was how to build a bridge that had very little rise to it (to accommodate the low-lying track bed), yet was still high enough to allow boats to pass underneath. His Maidenhead Bridge design is a work of true beauty. Two identical, long and flat arches span the river, somehow blending the architecture with the landscape. Designed almost 200 years ago, the bridge's sleek design has a modern look to it.

As a visionary, Brunel needed patience and understanding to convince people of the brilliance of his game-changing designs. The contractor who had been commissioned to build the Maidenhead Bridge was so alarmed when he saw Brunel's plans for the arches that he demanded the contract be immediately cancelled. He only acquiesced after Brunel explained the mathematics behind his design.

A worthy side note to the construction of the bridge: the board of the Great Western Railway believed that the two brick arches were so long and so flat that they would surely collapse if the wooden scaffolding used during their construction were ever to be removed. In fact, the wooden scaffolding ended just below the arches and bore no weight. An optical illusion made it appear as though the wood supported the archways, but when Brunel told the board members, they did not believe him. It wasn't until a flood washed away the scaffolding that the men finally trusted Brunel's design.

The Maidenhead Bridge brick archways remain to this day the widest and flattest in the world. Their strength has been tested each day since—modern high-speed and local trains pass over this bridge every five to ten minutes, 365 days per year.

Sonning Cutting: Another 11 miles (18 km) west from the Maidenhead Bridge lies the picturesque village of Sonning. It was here that Brunel encountered a hill that required cutting through to create a level train line. 1,200 men dug it out using pickaxes, shovels and wheelbarrows, with 200 horses used to haul away the rocks and soil. When the torrential rains in the autumn of 1839 turned the hillsides to mud and threatened to slow progress, Brunel took over managing the excavation, leading from the front and working sixteen hours per day. When the two-mile-long cutting (3.2 km) was finally completed in 1840, it facilitated Gooch's *Firefly* locomotive to reach a top speed of 50 miles per hour (80 km/h) between London and Reading.

Box Tunnel: This tunnel exemplifies more than anything Brunel's approach to complex engineering problems that others at the time wouldn't even attempt to solve. From the shape, size and consistency of the two-mile-long hill near the village of Box—70 miles (112 km) west of Sonning—Brunel knew that it could not be leveled. So, he planned to tunnel directly through it. No tunnel of this length had ever been attempted anywhere in the world.

That did not deter Brunel.

He planned for tunneling to begin on both the east and west sides simultaneously, meeting in the middle. The tunnel took five years to build and sadly took the lives of over 100 workers. Over 4,000 men worked on the tunnel, and more than one ton of explosives and one ton of candles for illumination were used each week. After five years of work and two miles of tunneling, the alignment was very nearly perfect. When the east and west teams met in the middle, they were off dead-center by only 2 inches (5 cm).

Box Tunnel was so long that passengers were fearful they'd suffocate going through it, so plans had to be made for trains to stop before the tunnel entrance to allow nervous passengers to transfer to horse-drawn carriages, and then reboard a later train on the other side. Brunel had foreseen the ventilation problem and during tunnel construction had six enormous air shafts dug through the top of Box Hill, but the traveling public were still initially anxious about this part of the journey.

Rumor had it that Brunel had allegedly designed the eastern entrance of the tunnel to align with the rising sun on his birthday each year, flooding the tunnel with a beam of sunlight. It was not until his birthday, April 9 in 2017, over 175 years after completion, that this was proven. Renovation of the train tracks that day had closed the tunnel to traffic. Fortunately, the closure coincided with a sunny day, enabling this phenomenon to be seen.[5]

Bristol Temple Meads Station: The crowning achievement of this magnificent Tudor-style station was the wooden roof, positioned over five sets of the Great Western Railway's wide-gauge train tracks. It covered the area where passengers boarded and disembarked trains. At the time of its construction, it was the widest single-span structure ever built.

The entire trainline was completed in 1841. In July through December of that first year of operation, Brunel's trains carried over 850,000 passengers.

The tracks, structures and trains were only part of the story. The real legacy was something much greater, and something you are unlikely to forget.

Chapter 6

The Great Western Railway's Dazzling Legacy

The legacy of the Great Western Railway is enormous. In addition to its many historic achievements, it enabled same-day connectivity between previously disparate parts of southwestern Great Britain and London. While such innovations were also occurring across Europe and America, this particular railway was leagues ahead, and set many of the standards all others would follow.

These epic elements included:

1. Upon completion, it was the longest and fastest railway in the world.

2. Brunel pioneered how high speed, inter-city rail is experienced today. Main line tracks connect major urban centers. To reach nearby towns and cities, we still board connecting trains at interchange stations, as Brunel had first envisioned.

3. There were many "firsts", including the creation of the longest tunnel through a hill (Box Tunnel), the widest side-supported wood span roof (Temple Meads Station), the widest and flattest brick arches ever built on any structure to this day (Maidenhead Bridge), and the largest train station roof of its era (Paddington Station).

While bridges existed long before railways were built, trains presented a bigger problem: how to cope with a heavy, sustained and vibrating load. Engineering had to evolve to develop bridges that could support the load, be affordable to build, and last for decades.

Brunel was a master bridge designer. His work, which involved experimenting with new materials for bridges and building roof spans over train stations, paved the way for greater, taller and stronger constructions. In addition to pioneering better bridge designs, he also had to develop innovative, bridge construction techniques where none existed before, to serve his purpose.

4. One of the more notable elements of the whole undertaking was that the structures of the Great Western Railway—the stations, tunnel entrances, and bridges (only a few of which are described in this chapter)—were designed using different architectural styles. Rather than choosing the easiest or the cheapest option, Brunel created a train line that would become a visual feast.

5. Brunel not only built the London-to-Bristol railway. He went on to design and build much of the railway network through to the farthest reaches of Cornwall in southwest England. This included the spectacular train line that runs along the southern English coast, right at the water's edge, on its way to Plymouth.

6. Locomotive engine technology also was improved. Daniel Gooch, who worked for Brunel, advanced locomotive design by years, improving steam to thrust capacity and enabling the Great Western Railway to deliver a more reliable high-speed service.

7. The route that Brunel surveyed for the London-to-Bristol railway, using only the optical and chain measure available

in his day, is very nearly the most level route one could attain. Modern topological maps, drone photography and satellite imagery probably could not have been able to significantly improve upon it. The proof is simply that today's high-speed London-to-Bristol trains travel on exactly the same route that Brunel had selected on horseback, almost two centuries ago!

That's only touching the surface of Isambard Kingdom Brunel's influence. Here are a few more epic elements.

Standardized time

An important part of the London-to-Bristol Great Western Railway's legacy is that it led to the development of standardized national time. It was the precursor to the establishment of Greenwich Mean Time (commonly referred to as GMT) and similar time zones that exist throughout the world today.

The main reason: The railway connected two major cities on an almost perfect east-west axis which made time more of an issue.

In the 1830s, time in all locations across major countries was determined by the rising sun. This was especially true in Britain. That meant the time in London was four minutes ahead of the time in Reading, situated 34 miles (55 km) to the west, and eleven minutes ahead of the time in Bristol, which was over 78 miles (125 km) west of Reading.

This had never posed a problem previously, because in this era, people travelled by horse and carriage. With the advent of better roads and stagecoach services enabling horse changes, the most one could comfortably travel in a day was about seventy miles and that would literally take all day. With Bristol being 116 miles from London, there was no way to travel that distance in a single day. A matter of minutes meant nothing in that sort of journey.

With Brunel's level track, trains could now travel at top speeds of 50 miles per hour (80 kph). Even if they averaged 30 mph (48 kph), it still meant that a passenger could get from London to Reading in about an hour, or London to Bristol in about four hours.

Now minutes meant something.

It was at the moment that the London-to-Bristol trainline was fully completed, and its fast trains enabled passengers to travel a very long distance in a few hours, that national time became important. The challenge that Brunel and the Great Western Railway faced was how to create a simple, uniform timetable that passengers, train drivers and conductors could all use to ensure on-time arrivals. These timetables were not just valuable to the traveling public. They also ensured that trains did not collide with each other.

The placing of the telegraph line alongside the railway line (a technique first pioneered on Brunel's Wharncliffe Viaduct) enabled the delivery of instant communication via a telegraphic code. This not only facilitated the sharing of information in real time, but allowed crucial information to be passed on to the train operators. For the first time ever, they would know when a train was coming, and if it was on time or running late. Because trains and telegraph communications were emerging at exactly the same time, this created a need to standardize not only time but a means of how to communicate it.

Catching criminals with the telegraph line

The railway and telegraph line had additional uses. With the advent of fast trains, criminals could now commit a crime in one area and escape to another part of the country with relative ease. The juxtaposition of the railway and telegraph line enabled police to take swift action against them.

The first occurrence of this happened during a large festive event in Slough, in 1844. Three men named Burrell, Sparrow and Spurgeon journeyed from London by train, robbed people at the event, and then boarded a train back to Paddington Station. Using the telegraph, local Slough police alerted their London counterparts to the men's descriptions and indicated which train carriage they were in. The three men were swiftly apprehended upon arrival.

In an even higher profile case in 1845, John Tawell poisoned his mistress in a small village near Slough on New Year's Day. Fleeing the crime scene, Tawell ran to the station and boarded a Great Western Railway train to London. It was quickly discovered that he was wearing a long, brown coat. A telegraph message was sent to Paddington Station with that detail, and Tawell was identified upon leaving the train.

It was both the first occurrence of a murderer escaping by train and the first capture of a murderer using intelligence conveyed across a high-tech apparatus. The British public was transfixed by the crime, the escape method used, the electric telegraph technology that helped catch him and the trial that ensued. Tawell was hung for his crime. Telegraphic communication grew in stature from that point, ultimately leading to the laying of a transatlantic communications cable twenty years later, which was another endeavor that Brunel influenced.

An even greater legacy

In the early days, the fabulous GWR railway came to be known as "God's Wonderful Railway." In more recent times, serious consideration was given to classify the entire Great Western Railway as a World Heritage Site, putting it in the same league as historical structures like the Taj Mahal and the Colosseum in Rome.[6]

As if this weren't enough, Brunel left us with an even more spectacular legacy, much greater than a railway connecting two British cities.

> Brunel dreamed of a transport link connecting London to New York City.

It may be worth reading that sentence again. Remember, he envisioned this at a time when people were still traveling by horse and carriage, and household electricity was still forty years away from being invented. Brunel's vision was to build a high-speed rail connection that would take passengers from the great city of London to the port city of Bristol. From there, they would board a "Great Western" ship to take them across the Atlantic to the fast-growing and exciting city of New York.

And who better to build that ship?

Isambard Kingdom Brunel, of course.

It would be the biggest ship ever built. Did he achieve this? We will save that for a later chapter.

What we can take from Brunel's vision and apply to our own projects:

- **Don't fear failure. Learn from it, and change course.** Brunel's long list of failures include locomotive designs that never lived up to expectations and track beds that made for uncomfortable journeys. He tried hard to make the ideas work, but when it became clear something wasn't working, Brunel re-examined the problem and tried another approach. This valuable strategy is as effective today as it was in the 19th century.

- **If someone asks for one design why not give them four?** For the Avon Gorge Bridge, Brunel presented four designs to the Bristol political leaders—three more than the other contenders provided. This bold approach impressed the Bristol political leaders and won Brunel the job. This lateral approach could be applied to everything from designing your own garden, to developing new product launch plans, to submitting ideas for an article to a magazine (as one of us discovered only recently).

- **'Tunnel' through obstacles.** It's likely Brunel looked at the hill at Box and thought, "So what if we have to tunnel through it and it will take five years and it has never been done before? Why should that stop me?" Seeking routes through obstacles, not around them, could lead to more direct solutions.

- **Think from the customer's point of view.** We might imagine Brunel thinking: "It's not just a station; it's an opportunity to improve passenger comfort. It's not just a group of train stations; it's a visual display of architectural styles. It's not just a viaduct, it's a structure to support the newly created electronic telegraph wires that will transform how communication works." Envisioning the entire customer experience can lead to better future interactions.

- **Think audaciously.** When tackling a project, can you think of it not as "London-to-Bristol" but as "London-to-New York?"

How the Great Western Railway looks for today's travelers

The entire line and all the bridges, viaducts and tunnels that Brunel created exist today largely as he designed them—a testament to his immense engineering ability. As you travel from London Paddington Station all the way to Bristol Temple Meads Station you can experience the magnificent structures Brunel built along the way.

The roof of Paddington Station has not been altered since it was first erected. The magnificent Wharncliffe Viaduct at Hanwell also remains intact, though it has since been widened to accommodate more tracks. If you get off at Hanwell station, there is a scenic walk you can take around and under the Viaduct. Maidenhead Bridge, 1.4 miles (2.2 km) from Maidenhead station, is a wonder to see. The bridge was widened in the 1890's for the addition of two tracks, but the structure still looks the same. When riding on the GWR train to Bristol, you still travel through the Sonning Cutting and Box Tunnel.

Brunel's Bristol Temple Meads Station still exists, but is no longer used as a train station. Train travel through this station became so popular that by 1870, a larger Gothic style station had to be built next to it. For a long time, the original train shed roof that Brunel designed unceremoniously covered part of a station car park. Recently it has been restored and converted into a wedding and events venue. (If you do get to Bristol, it is worth visiting Brunel's picturesque Clifton Suspension Bridge over the Avon Gorge. This bridge design helped bring Brunel to the attention of the Bristol city officials.)

The locomotives from Brunel's era can be viewed in various railway museums across the UK. Stephenson's *Rocket* is in the National Railway Museum in York. A model of Gooch's *Firefly* locomotive is in the London Science Museum.

And fittingly, there is a statue of Brunel between platforms 8 and 9 of London Paddington Station.

If Isambard Kingdom Brunel left behind a monumental legacy, the subject of our next chapters, Theodore Roosevelt, undertook endeavors of a different kind. Along the way, Roosevelt made enemies, one of whom owned a gun.

Part Two

Daring Greatly: Theodore Roosevelt

The Statesman

"Death had to take him sleeping, for if Roosevelt had been awake, there would have been a fight."

—*Thomas Marshall, US Vice President, 1919*

Chapter 7

Even A Bullet Couldn't Stop Him

A man jumps out in front of the former president, brandishing a pistol. He aims it and pulls the trigger, shooting fifty-three-year-old Theodore Roosevelt in the chest. It is October 14, 1912.

Roosevelt was leaving his hotel at the time, on his way to give a campaign speech at the Milwaukee Auditorium. He was running for president of the United States a second time, this time representing the upstart Progressive Party (also known as the Bull Moose Party). The bullet, slowed by his steel glasses case and the fifty-page speech he carried in his breast pocket, still penetrated Roosevelt's chest.

What did Roosevelt do next: Collapse in a heap? Go to the hospital? Cower behind armed guards inside the safety of the hotel?

None of these things.

With the bullet still lodged in his chest and blood seeping from the wound, Roosevelt went to the auditorium and gave his speech.

His opening words were, "Friends, I shall ask you to be as quiet as possible. I don't know whether you fully understand that I have just been shot." Opening his jacket and showing the crowd his red-stained shirt, he said, "It takes more than that to kill a bull moose."[7]

Theodore Roosevelt was a force of nature. A mere bullet was not going to stop him. He was the youngest man to ever become president in 1901 (at age forty-two) and served in the office admirably for the next eight years. Having watched his successor William Taft's performance in the White House, Roosevelt decided the time had come to campaign for a second time to become president.

As a sickly child in a wealthy family, it would have been easier for the asthmatic Roosevelt to stay home and indulge his interest in animals, birds and taxidermy. Instead, he evolved to become one of the most interesting Americans to have ever lived.[8]

Roosevelt was far from perfect—his mistakes were many—but the accomplishments of his two terms in the presidency (1901-1909) were remarkable. Among them were the expansion of the US National Park and National Forest systems, which became a model for land and wildlife conservation around the world. Roosevelt also championed the construction of the Panama Canal, which accelerated international commerce and transformed the way goods are shipped around the globe. His successes here were all the more notable because his critics believed nothing significant could be accomplished in those areas.

Roosevelt's personal transformation from a rich and pampered boy who was bullied in his early years, to one of the toughest men who has proven his strength in the political arena, on the battlefield, and on the frontier lands of the western United States is only part of the story. All his life he strove for lasting acts of greatness in the face of what others thought to be unattainable goals.

On October 14, 1912, with the bullet still in his chest and blood soaking his shirt, Roosevelt gave a speech lasting well over an hour (eighty-four minutes to be precise). Given the enormous successes he had achieved already in his life, it is little wonder that a bullet could not stop him.

His famous bloodied shirt, glasses case, and the fifty-page manuscript of his Milwaukee speech are in a museum fittingly run by the National Park Service, an organization developed a few years after Roosevelt's presidency ended.

While reading about the vast tracts of land Roosevelt helped to protect during his presidency, and the magnitude of the challenges in building the Panama Canal—both detailed in this section—you may want to think about this:

What cause would drive you so strongly that even a bullet could not stop you from pursuing it?

Arches National Park.

Chapter 8
Seizing Opportunities

The Origins Of Our World's Conservation Movement

Theodore Roosevelt's impact on our modern world was immense. Before we delve into his lasting achievements, it would first be helpful to step back in time to examine what drove him to become the "man in the arena" as part of his famous quote explains.

To be the one, *"...whose face is marred by dust and sweat and blood; who strives valiantly; who errs, who comes short again and again ... who at the best knows in the end the triumph of high achievement, and who at the worst, if he fails, at least fails while daring greatly ..."* [9]

Some passions hit us early in life, and once nurtured never depart.

Theodore Roosevelt's love for wildlife and the great outdoors must have started early on, probably as soon as he could read. The Roosevelt brownstone home in New York City's Gramercy Park had a library with a wide range of books—the hallmark of a family bent on nurturing a life of investigation and study. One of these books was *The Boy Hunters*, a young-adult novel from 1853. It was filled with exciting tales of outdoor adventure intended to inspire its readers to study nature.

With Roosevelt, the book appeared to have attained its goal. The heroes of the overwrought prose were a group of boys living alone in the wilderness, hunting to feed themselves, sleeping under buffalo robes and exploring the vast open land that stretched across America. According to its author, Mayne Reid, America's interior was rich and beautiful, but he warned it was also ripe to be exploited by capitalist "king vultures," ready to swoop down and prey upon the poor and defenseless.

Many of us may have had a book like that from our childhoods, something we read over and over until it fell apart, and whose influence shaped our lives. In that respect, Theodore Roosevelt was one of us. Inspired by Reid's storytelling and the books of the American ornithologist John James Audubon and other leading naturalists of the day, Theodore was encouraged to pursue his studies and follow wherever they led him. His father was one of the original founders of the American Museum of Natural History, and young Roosevelt following his example aspired to one day have a museum of his own.

It started in the library, on the top floor of the multi-story family home, where young Theodore was given a shelf on which to store and catalog his growing collection. His original charter of the *Roosevelt Museum of Natural History*—five pages handwritten by his ten-year-old self—declared its official opening with a display of twelve specimens. By the end of the year his collection had grown to 250 specimens—birds' nests, mouse skeletons, dead insects and seashells—anything that caught his interest and required further study.

His varied interest narrowed to bird study by the age of fourteen, during a family vacation on the Nile. He reframed the trip to Egypt as the *Official scientific expedition for the collection of specimens for the Roosevelt Museum of Natural History*.

Once there, he ventured far afield from the rest of the family, seeking new birds to add to his collection, and making notes on their habitats to add to his essay called, *The Ornithology of Egypt between Cairo and Assuan*.[10] Although he might have been too young to be considered a scientist in January of 1873, his aspiration as revealed on this trip showed he had an already oversized ambition for it.

His parents may have hoped that *The Boy Hunters* book would have engaged and entertained their son and, perhaps, led him to the love of study and literature. They could hardly have imagined how that one book's influence would be the source material for many of Roosevelt's achievements over the course of his vigorous life.

"Life is a great adventure ... accept it in such a spirit."[11]
—*Theodore Roosevelt*

Imagine if his parents had not had that particular book in the house?

Neither of them lived long enough to see the start of his impactful career in public life, which ultimately led to the establishment of the National Park Service by a later president. The path Roosevelt's career took was of his own making, and the steps along it, of his own choosing.

Roosevelt's path to greatness was not a straight course by any means. While his choices eventually led him to become President of the United States, his first steps were not driven by political ambition, but by a desire to live life to the fullest in the broad reaches of the great outdoors.

His childhood asthma cleared up. Roosevelt believed it happened because he embraced a strenuous exercise routine in his teenage years. Driven by the mental and physical stimulation he got from hiking with his family, he took up other vigorous activities such as boxing.

Roosevelt's interests also evolved. He abandoned his plan for an academic career in natural science and replaced it with the desire to become a political reformer. He enrolled in Columbia Law School, and while there, married Alice Hathaway Lee. But he quickly became bored with the study of law, spending his time instead doing research for the first of the many books he would write. His first book, *Naval War of 1812*, replete with arcane details of ship maneuvers and cannon fire techniques, brought the different leadership styles between Britain's Royal Navy and its American counterpart to his attention.

The study, and the writing, set his active mind in motion. While most of his wealthy, young friends carefully avoided politics lest it damage their prospects, he dove into politics head first. Taking up the mantle of the Republican Party in 1882, Roosevelt was elected to represent Manhattan in the New York State Assembly. Here his desire to protect the average person against corporate corruption—first inspired by his childhood reading of *The Boy Hunters*—began to reveal itself publicly. His outspoken anti-corruption work led to his re-election in 1883 by a two-to-one margin, and again in 1884.

It was during his second term that Roosevelt first visited the wide open, buffalo-covered plains of the Dakota Territory and got a taste for the open air, rough-and-tumble life of the cowboy. Here his childhood dream blossomed from fantasy into a life-changing reality. Seeing an opportunity to combine business and pleasure, he invested $14,000 (about $350,000 in today's money) in a cattle ranch named after the eight-pointed Maltese Cross used on its livestock branding iron.

Within a year he had started to build a ranch of his own a little farther out in the wild. He spent the next two years happily shuttling back and forth from the state capitol in Albany, New York, to the ranch, until tragedy struck.

In a double blow when Roosevelt was just twenty-six years old, his mother and his 22 year old wife both died in separate events on Valentine's Day, 1884. While his mother's death had been expected, his wife's, mere days after giving birth, had not.

Devastated, he wrote in his diary that night, "The light has gone out of my life."

He could not bear to live in such darkness. He returned to Albany to finish his term as assemblyman, and later in the year decided to go back to the open plains of North Dakota. Leaving his newborn daughter (who was named Alice, after her mother) in the care of his sister Anna, Roosevelt headed to his newly built Elkhorn Ranch to grieve.

It was here in the remote and windswept plains that he found solace, and began his writing career in earnest, starting with magazine articles and the first three of his books on the life of an outdoorsman: *Hunting Trips of a Ranchman, Ranch Life and the Hunting-Trail,* and *The Wilderness Hunter.*

Combining two loves: politics and nature

The three books cemented Roosevelt's reputation as an erstwhile New York reformer who had swapped politics and urban life for the great outdoors. This gave him a platform from which to proclaim his newfound conservationist ideas. His interest in big-game hunting evolved as well—shifting from the wanton killing of wild animals to the desire to protect habitats and promote fair chase hunting.

With the help of his influential friend, the naturalist and writer George Bird Grinnell, Roosevelt recognized that the United States government's laissez-faire approach was stripping the nation of its natural resources—from the forests and prairies, to the large and small game that called them home—and bending to market forces keen on exploiting them for short-term profits. It would require someone with a longer-term vision to help preserve these natural resources for future use and enjoyment.

The American conservationist movement, which Roosevelt was now associated with, was less concerned with keeping the wilderness in pristine condition and untouched by human development than it was with preparing it for continued, sustainable use across many generations in the future. The art and science of forestry was coming into its own, combining the principles of biology and chemistry with the applied sciences of ecology and resource management. Archaeology was also coming into play as remnants of early human cultures, discovered on lands under government control, were becoming increasingly important to the recording and appreciation of human history throughout the Americas.

Eventually, Roosevelt realized that if he truly wanted the

conservationist movement to succeed, he would have to expand his influential reach beyond that of his current role as a part-time gentleman rancher in the Dakota Territory.

His attempted return to political life ended in defeat in 1886, after an unsuccessful run for mayor of New York City. He retreated to his ranch and focused his efforts on another book (actually a four-volume series, never quite completed), *The Winning of the West*. This project combined two of his greatest intellectual loves: American history and the exploration of the vast wilderness lying between the Mississippi River and the Pacific Ocean.

Joining forces with other like-minded visionaries, Roosevelt, Grinnell, Gifford Pinchot and twenty-one others, co-founded the Boone and Crockett Club. (Today, it is America's oldest wildlife conservation organization.)

Although Roosevelt's career trajectory played right into the development of a National Park system, that was not his goal—at least not at first. The first National Park had been established years before at Yellowstone, by President Ulysses S. Grant. Yellowstone consisted of vast, strikingly unusual acreage featuring geysers and hot springs in the Wyoming and Montana territories. Sequoia and Yosemite were the next two National Parks to be established. Both were created in 1890.

With no government service dedicated to their protection and administration, these parks were left in the care of the US Army. The army, however, had other weightier matters to contend with. Lax supervision allowed poachers, illegal tree felling operators and grazing animals to run rampant.

Roosevelt vowed to take action. Working alongside other founders, the Boone and Crockett Club's intensive lobbying helped to bring about the passage of the Yellowstone Game Protection Act of 1894, the first law of its kind regulating the conduct of hunters and developers in any national park—but applied only in that one park. For Roosevelt though, it was a personal mark of achievement that left him hungry for more. To achieve his new goals, he would have to go back into politics in a more serious way.

The rise of the reformer

Roosevelt's reputation was growing. President Benjamin Harrison hired Roosevelt as civil service commissioner. In this new posting to Washington D.C., Roosevelt found that he could buck the established bureaucracy and bring about reforms, in spite of formidable opposition. But his new wife, Edith Roosevelt, did not want him returning to politics. At her request he declined an offer to run for mayor of New York.

Disheartened by Edith's opposition to politics, Roosevelt retreated to his ranch, but a new posting as New York City Police Commissioner in 1894 brought him back to political life. As head of the police Roosevelt instituted long-needed reforms, such as recruiting and advancement based on merit rather than political affiliation, and rooting out corruption in the department. He took to walking the city streets late at night to make sure the patrolmen were on the beat.

Roosevelt also became friends with the journalist Jacob Riis, who wrote a widely read essay titled, *How the Other Half Lives*. In it, Riis documented with graphic, hard-hitting photographs the intense squalor of the New York City slums and tenement buildings. Riis' pioneering work helped revive Roosevelt's sense of moral purpose that had first been lit by the childhood books he'd read.

While the Police Commission post had nothing to do with conservation, and kept him away from his beloved North Dakota ranch, it bolstered his reputation as a public figure willing to stick his neck out to defend the rights of the common man. This in turn led to his emergence as a national figure.

Leading from the front

By the time of the outbreak of the Spanish–American War in 1898, Roosevelt was working in President McKinley's administration as Assistant Secretary of the Navy. A strong advocate for Cuban independence, Roosevelt could have remained in Washington and helped from there, but the lure of adventure and bringing aid to the downtrodden was too great to resist. Swiftly responding to the President's call for a ground force of 125,000 volunteers, Roosevelt resigned his position and raised a regiment of "Rough Riders," making sure they would go into battle with the best of equipment. And the best of leadership.

Roosevelt led from the front. He asked no one to take any risk he was not willing to take himself. (This was a trait he shared with Brunel and Amundsen.)

In the absence of a ranking officer at the Battle of San Juan Hill, Roosevelt took control of his men and gave the order to storm the hill. Mounting his horse, he charged to the front of the battle line and, waving his sword, led the troops to victory. His gallantry in this battle ensured him widespread respect and recognition that would later see him elected governor of the state of New York in 1898.

At the Republican national convention in 1900, Roosevelt accepted the nomination to run as Vice President in William McKinley's second presidential bid. Although he had once considered and then rejected his own run at the presidency, he took on his new role with gusto. Always the tireless campaigner, Roosevelt traveled from location to location that autumn, by a specially outfitted train, to make 480 speeches in twenty-three states.

The pair won the election easily.

In March 1901, Roosevelt was sworn in as Vice President. But it soon became apparent that this seemingly powerless role did not sit well with his outgoing, assertive temperament.

The abrupt assassination of McKinley a mere six months later changed everything for Roosevelt. It was originally thought that McKinley, who had been speaking at the Pan-American Exposition in Buffalo, New York would survive, so Roosevelt continued traveling in the days following the shooting. But at a railroad station in North Creek, New York, Roosevelt learned that President McKinley had died eight days after being shot.

Thanks to Brunel's pioneering railroad development, by 1901

rail travel had long been the most efficient way to travel between cities. A special train brought Roosevelt straight to Buffalo. There, on September 14, 1901, Theodore Roosevelt was sworn in as the 26th president of the United States. He then went by train to Washington DC and soon moved into the Executive Mansion with his wife Edith and their six children. Roosevelt later renamed it as the White House.

Theodore Roosevelt's varied career thus far had prepared him well for the role. Public life is not for everyone and only suits those with a strong will and sense of purpose. For every person who agrees with that purpose there will be another who vehemently disagrees, in word and deed. Complete strangers will become friends to gain access to those in power; others will become enemies, using their constitutional right to free speech for slander and defamation. Some go so far as to carry out assassination attempts to achieve their ends.

Roosevelt faced all of these ploys.

Chapter 9

Preserving Nature And Wildlife On A Grand Scale

Before he became president, Theodore Roosevelt had spent years watching helplessly as plunderers eviscerated the natural world around him, taking full advantage of the lack of laws protecting it.

The American plains, once home to thirty million buffalo and where antelope had roamed freely, had been given over to agriculture—decimating grazing land and animal populations. Across this broad landscape, once-plentiful birds now faced extinction due to their vanishing habitats. But there was an even more serious concern, and it was threatening to devastate the bird population faster than agriculture.

The feather trade.

At the turn of the twentieth century, demand for feathers was high. Millinery, or the ladies' hat trade, needed a supply of colorful, soft feathers which would be used to artfully embellish the hats of the rich. It wasn't long before a lucrative black market arose, enabling the selling of the colorful feathers of Florida's most exotic birds.

The rural "plumers" may not have realized that some birds were literally worth their weight in gold. The most successful of these hunters bagged 10,000 birds in a season, sending the skins north to

New York, along with the most desirable carcasses that would end up in the finest Manhattan restaurants.

Millions of birds were wiped out in the name of this "gilded age" of fashion. Unless a countermovement started that was willing to publicly shame such wanton, showy extravagance, the plumers would continue unabated.

It was around the same time that ornithology, the branch of zoology dealing with birds, became popular. The women's suffrage movement was also beginning to make headway and advocated often for the rights of birds, regularly filling the halls for Frank Chapman's "Woman as a Bird Enemy" lectures. (Chapman was the leading ornithologist at the American Museum of Natural History.) All of this reinforced the need for a change.

President Roosevelt takes charge

The year before his assassination, President McKinley had signed the Lacey Act into law, named after Congressman John Fletcher Lacey. The law protected birds from illegal interstate commerce. Roosevelt had known Lacey since the early 1890s, and was a longtime supporter of his conservationist ideas. Now that Roosevelt was president, with politically connected friends and allies like Lacey, he was in a better position to lead the charge in fighting the feather trade.

Thrust into the role earlier than expected and in charge of the executive branch of the US government, Roosevelt set about expanding the power of the president's office. Armed with ideas and plans of his own he wasted no time in seeking to implement them.

He laid them out in his first annual message to Congress in December 1901, mere months after assuming the presidency. The country was still reeling from the assassination of McKinley, seeing it as an assault on the nation's values. In his address, Roosevelt laid out his vision for the United States, including his plans for the vast reserves of forests spreading across the western states. These forests would be carefully nurtured to become an everlasting resource of timber and recreational land, as well as habitats for all types of animals and birds.

In that first message Roosevelt did not ask Congress for game and forest protection—he *demanded* it. He had plans and scientific ideas to be brought into play. Congressional lawmakers resisted at first, but Roosevelt kept hammering his points home until his ideas took seed and wildlife conservation bore fruit on a grand, national scale.

Like Brunel before him and Amundsen after, Theodore Roosevelt understood that innovative ideas and big plans would never become realities unless he put his own considerable energy into it, brought in the right team and didn't stop pushing forward.

Even though Presidents Grant, Harrison and McKinley had created the four national parks then existing in the United States (Yellowstone, Sequoia, Yosemite and Mount Ranier), Roosevelt's other presidential predecessors had shown little interest in defending the natural resources of the United States. Rampant extraction and wanton destruction of the nation's reserves by businesses pursuing short-term profit continued unabated, and they took no responsibility for the devastation they caused.

Roosevelt saw himself as the frontline defender of these resources, irrespective of the political outcome. It would require his best strategic thinking to make it a reality.

He began his efforts slowly, starting with just a couple of forest preserves in states where he knew the political opposition would be reliably minimal. Then, having set a precedent, he moved more assertively, knowing that if he was successful in his re-election, he would be in an excellent position to move fast, to make happen what he knew was best for the nation's future.

In addition to his numerous executive actions, Roosevelt led the three-year political fight to pass the Forest Transfer Act of 1905 and the Forest Homestead Act of 1906, defending both the rational use and conservation of the nation's forests. While many valuable forests had already passed into private hands, much remained public and needed protection.

Roosevelt refused to let the opportunity slip away.

When the Transfer Act was signed into law, it enabled him to issue a remarkable 370 Forest Reserve proclamations during the remaining years of his second term. This amounted to a staggering 194 million acres of protected land. To give you a perspective, if you grouped all of the National Forests in the United States together, they would cover an area larger than the entire land mass of France, the Netherlands and Belgium. In a US context, this is more than one third of the size of the enormous Louisiana Purchase.

The Forest Homestead Act ensured that every tract within the forests that was suitable for agriculture remained available to pioneering farmers wishing to live on it and turn the raw land into working farms. The newly organized Forest Rangers served to protect not only the government's interest in the forests but the safety and welfare of the growing number of citizens who visited them recreationally.

It takes this kind of assertive, direct action to make big things happen. Roosevelt was not averse to using sharp, political means to achieve his end goals (a skill that became increasingly important in his work on the Panama Canal as well). The Supreme Court upheld all but one of his many executive actions for conservation.

His success with the Forest Service laid the foundation for his next mission:

Taking federal control of the archaeological sites that dotted the country, from one end to the other. The aim was to preserve the remnants of the great civilizations that had once thrived on the American continent before the coming of the Europeans.

The power of Roosevelt's Antiquities Act

That early family vacation to Egypt had reinforced not only Roosevelt's scientific interest in birds and wildlife and their habitat, but also his interest in the archaeological remains of long-vanished societies. This interest blossomed further during his undergraduate days at Harvard.

People knew archaeological sites existed in the United States but little was known about the indigenous populations they belonged to, and even less respect was given to them. Multiple areas across the United States abounded with rock drawings, cave dwellings, abandoned pueblos, shell mounds and remains of decorated pottery and textiles, especially in the desert regions of the Southwest, where isolation and dry climate preserved them.

These sites of national interest were under constant threat from artifact-hunters, willing to pillage for their wealthy patrons. All over the southwestern United States the fragile remnants of past civilizations were being dug up and displaced, or sold. The President was keenly aware of this ongoing practice. It was Congressman Lacey who helped Roosevelt to think beyond the preservation of the nation's natural resources and to expand his vision to include the protection of archaeological sites on public lands.

But Congress of 1906–1908 did not agree with Roosevelt's presidential overreach, and had hoped to use Lacey's friendship with him to temper it.

They reasoned that if Roosevelt got his way with the Antiquities Act, Lacey could convince him to back off from imposing more restrictions on developing forests and other government-owned lands. Powerful developers with the ear of Congress also hoped that by giving Roosevelt a couple of hundred acres of archaeological sites in the desert, the president would in return help them get a free hand to make money from land elsewhere.

They were wrong.

The Antiquities Act of 1906, an incredible and enduring piece of legislation, became a formidable weapon in Roosevelt's hands. It gave him (and any future president) the power to declare any US monument anywhere as national, and protected in the country's best interest. Roosevelt achieved this by utilizing the clause in the Act that gave him presidential *discretion* over anything that could be considered "historical landmarks, historic preservation structures, and other objects of scientific interest."

Thanks to Lacey, Roosevelt was able to add "scenic and scientific" elements into the legislation, greatly expanding the Act's reach. The law obligated federal agencies managing public lands to preserve them for present and future generations. Roosevelt used this legislation to great effect to protect vast tracts of land.

How vast?

The numbers, as shown in the next chapter, are astonishing.

Chapter 10

A Legacy Of Conservation

Theodore Roosevelt's conservation legacy is immense, both in what he created during his time in office, and what has happened since his presidency—not just on a US national level but on a global level.

By actions taken during his presidency alone, Roosevelt preserved 230 million acres (930,000 square km), roughly equivalent to the combined land mass of France, Germany and Switzerland, and more land than the entire original thirteen US states occupy today.

Impact in America

Roosevelt created or enlarged 150 national forests. This represents ninety-seven percent of all the national forests that exist in the United States today.

One of Roosevelt's early acts as president was to establish Pelican Island in Florida as the first Federal Bird Reservation. He went on to establish fifty similar reserves across the United States. These evolved into the National Wildlife Refuge System.

Roosevelt's leadership saved the lives of millions of birds and prevented species from being hunted into extinction. The National

Wildlife Refuge System has grown tenfold since Roosevelt first created the blueprint for it. The system now manages over 550 wildlife sites.

Roosevelt also created four national game preserves including the National Bison Range in Montana. This act saved the American Bison, an iconic and majestic animal of the US western frontier, from extinction.

Roosevelt's actions established six national parks and eighteen national monuments. Perhaps these numbers don't seem as large as the number of national forests or federal bird reserves, but they represent some of the US's most breathtaking and stunning terrains, landscapes and historical sites including Crater Lake, Oregon; Mesa Verde, Colorado (preserving Pueblo Indian cliff dwellings); the Petrified Forest, Arizona; Muir Woods, California; Natural Bridges, Utah; and the spectacular Grand Canyon.

Next time you visit any US National Monument or National Park—including the greatest of them all, the Grand Canyon—say thank you to Theodore Roosevelt for signing the Antiquities Act, the crowning achievement of his preservationist legacy.

The greatest effect of this far-reaching policy can be seen in the millions of acres that continue to remain as publicly owned land, maintained by the federal government for the use and benefit of US citizens. Subsequent administrations succeeded in creating the National Park Service, an agency dedicated to managing the parks and monuments.

It all happened because of President Theodore Roosevelt's lifelong dedication to the preservation of wildlife and open spaces, and making them a respected, enduring heritage of the nation.

And that's only part of the legacy.

International impact

Roosevelt's work had international importance. The land and wildlife conservation methods developed by Roosevelt provided a sound model for other countries seeking similar results.

National parks now exist in over 120 countries around the world. Australia has over 500 national parks, and thirty-eight percent of Belize is designated as national park land. Northeast Greenland is under preservation as the world's largest national park, covering 375,000 square miles (972,000 square km).

The value of national parks cannot be overstated.

They are a source of national pride; they protect important and diverse wildlife habitats around the world; they minimize the destruction of land, forests and species; and they increase awareness of the vital role that land, wildlife and climate play in everyone's lives.

National parks preserve cultures, civilizations, ruins and remains and archaeological heritage, and can serve as open-air teaching environments. In an increasingly urbanized population, they provide much needed recreational spaces, strengthen our ties to nature and provide a valuable glimpse into the wonders of the planet.

In addition, national parks can help improve water and air quality, protect endangered water supplies, and encourage sound land and water management practices. The parks protect land, while making it available in sustainable ways to tourism—a multi-billion-dollar industry.

It would not have been possible to do this on such a grand scale had Roosevelt not led the way in showing how a government can use legislative power for the common good, and preserve nature's bounty for future generations to enjoy.

Climate importance

Climate change is one of the most vital issues of our lifetime, highlighting the importance of land preservation, habitat, and forest and wildlife protection to our future as a species. Some national parks serve as research laboratories for assessing the impact of climate change. The shape of our world now and in the future is dependent on how we handle climate change.

Roosevelt knew this instinctively, almost one hundred years before many other politicians did. He could foresee the devastation that unbridled and unmanaged land development would bring. The Boone and Crockett Club he founded with Pinchot and Grinnell in 1887 is possibly the oldest land and wildlife protection organization in the world. It set the stage for the national and global conservation societies operating today, including World Wildlife Fund, Greenpeace, Sierra Club, the Nature Conservancy and many others.

But Theodore Roosevelt's vision didn't end there.

Like Isambard Kingdom Brunel, Roosevelt had an interest in railroads. While Brunel viewed railways as a means to connect cities, Roosevelt saw them as a way to connect Americans with nature. It is still possible to travel to US National Parks like Crater Lake, Glacier, Grand Canyon, Olympic, Rocky Mountain, and Yosemite on trains with exotic names like *Coast Starlight*, *Empire Builder* and *California Zephyr*.

Theodore Roosevelt set the legislative framework for how modern politicians can respond to climate change today. We must note, though, that the authors of this book do not revere Roosevelt for every decision he made. His behavior toward Native Americans (once in the White House he tried to make some amends, but certainly not enough), his remarks and writings favoring white people descended from Europeans, and his excessive hunting of animals, made for difficult reading during our research. But Roosevelt's environmental efforts and focus do deserve attention. For all his faults and all his accomplishments, he literally was the "man in the arena." His faults and successes are on display because he inserted himself into the action time and again.

The conservation movement that we know today largely comes down to one man: Theodore Roosevelt.

What can we learn from Roosevelt about leadership and commitment

- See it/Seize it: When an opportunity presents itself, grab it with both hands. Roosevelt did not seek to be president, but when McKinley's untimely assassination thrust the role upon him, he embraced the challenge. Often in life unplanned events will happen, and suddenly an opportunity—or challenge disguised as an opportunity— can arise. Recognize it, just as Roosevelt did, and strive to make the most of the opportunity.

- **Passion is contagious.** Roosevelt had a love for the natural world. He spoke eloquently on ways to preserve the landscapes, as well as the habitats and wildlife that existed on it. Conveying passion for his work, and life in general, generated enthusiasm in others, and helped him win over adversaries.

- **Small "wins" can generate momentum and build toward greater success.** Protecting large tracts of land across the United States began with Roosevelt first protecting smaller tracts, and learning along the way the methods needed to win wider, political support for his ideas. Small, definable wins can also help you or your business to gain momentum.

- **You don't have to agree on every issue to build solid, working relationships.** Roosevelt was an incredibly skilled statesperson. He learned and nurtured the art of how to create allies among a diverse range of people. His skill, which can also be applied today, was recognizing that people did not need to agree with him on every issue to win general support for specific projects.

- **Stay curious and continually learn about the world around you.** Roosevelt's deep understanding of the natural world and America's West meant that once he attained a position of power, he already knew where the problems lay and how to fix them. This insight allowed him to form tight governmental policies, while remaining open to learning more. The more he gleaned from multiple sources the greater the diversity of thought he was able to bring to his grand endeavors, and the more successful they became.

What you can see today

The sheer number of national parks, national monuments and national forests in the United States, and around the world, is staggering. Together they contain the most diversified collection of preserved land in the world, and you can visit them all. Many books, travel guides and websites are dedicated to helping you get the most from your time there.

One of these parks is the Theodore Roosevelt National Park, situated in western North Dakota. Included within its borders is Roosevelt's Maltese Cross Ranch. His childhood home in New York City is now a National Park Service site, as is his home at Sagamore Hill on Long Island, New York.

The American Museum of Natural History in New York City houses some of Roosevelt's early specimen collection from the *Roosevelt Museum of Natural History* which he created as a boy. The museum also features a Theodore Roosevelt Memorial Hall, which includes a bronze sculpture of Roosevelt dressed in his outdoor clothing. Set into the floor in front of the sculpture is a large medallion depicting an American bison and the words, "There can be no greater issue than that of conservation in this country." The excerpt is from Roosevelt's speech given ten weeks before a gunman shot, but did not kill him, in Milwaukee.

Conservation was only one of Roosevelt's grand legacies. Before we turn to another major accomplishment that helped solidify his credentials as a statesman, we should mention that Theodore Roosevelt never liked the nickname *Teddy*, which is why it is not used it in this book.

The nickname arose after an unsuccessful bear hunting trip that Roosevelt took in Mississippi, during the second year of his presidency. His trips attracted so much media attention, organizers thought it would look bad if the president, a keen hunter, didn't shoot at least one bear. So they caught a bear and restrained it, then encouraged Roosevelt to shoot it. Roosevelt, who only believed in fair chase hunting, declined.

The event was memorialized by a leading cartoonist at the time. Morris and Rose Michtom, an enterprising husband and wife team who made children's stuffed animals that they sold in their candy shop in Brooklyn, New York, saw the widely publicized cartoon and started making stuffed "Teddy Bears." The bear became so popular it led them to establish the Ideal Novelty and Toy Company (shortened to the Ideal Toy Company). Years later, Ideal would become most famous for popularizing the Rubik's Cube and the Magic 8 Ball—toys that some readers may remember fondly from their childhoods, before the company was sold to Mattel and Hasbro.

Roosevelt, however, felt that the Teddy nickname was unbecoming to the seriousness and stature of his presidency, and declined to use it. This sense of purpose was exemplified by a spectacular enterprise that Roosevelt set in motion: the building of the Panama Canal. Roosevelt knew that, if successful, the canal would reshape international commerce, the global economy and a new world order.

How it came into existence is a story you will never forget.

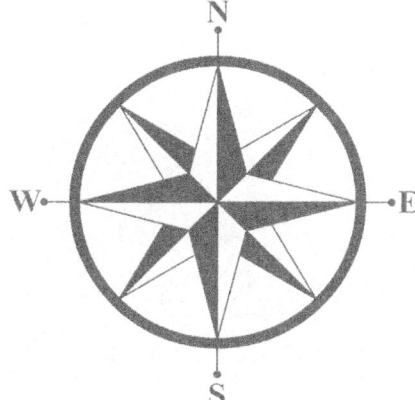

"Nothing in this world is worth having or worth doing unless it means effort, pain, difficulty."

—*Theodore Roosevelt*

Panama Canal today.

Chapter 11
Solving The Right Problem

The Waterway That Accelerated Global Trade

When it came to the Panama Canal, the issues facing President Roosevelt were not new ones. From the earliest times that Europeans and Asians started trading, politicians, explorers and engineers thought about how to speed up travel between their lands. Long, risky journeys were first made overland—think Marco Polo on the Silk Road in 1295—and later by ship, sailing a route first pioneered in 1497 by the explorer Vasco da Gama, around southern Africa.

Only a few years after da Gama, a new option emerged. Gold may have been the motivator for the Spanish explorer Balboa as he and his team trekked into the rainforest in 1513, of what is today known as Panama. But he discovered something of far greater value than gold: a vast sea on the far side of that narrow stretch of land, only 50 miles (80 km) from the Atlantic Ocean. He named that ocean Pacific, and almost from that very point in time, people dreamed of an interoceanic waterway to connect the two great seas.

Even in the 1500s, the value was clear. If achieved, no longer would European trade with the Far East require ships, laden with valued goods, to sail the long and treacherous routes below Africa or South America to reach their destinations—journeys that could take many months. No natural waterway across the isthmus of Panama could be found, so in 1534 King Charles V of Spain ordered a survey to determine the feasibility of building a canal. He was the first, but by no means the last to do so.

Envisioning a waterway across this part of Latin America and actually building one were quite different matters. Even centuries later, in the 1800s, no one could anticipate how challenging it would be to execute.

By the time Roosevelt came on the scene in the early 1900s, it was deemed nearly impossible, for reasons revealed below.

Engineering or politics?

One might think that building the canal was primarily an engineering problem.

Roosevelt and others certainly made this mistake initially, thinking the solution was about finding the best path, making use of as many of the existing rivers, lakes and natural harbors as possible and digging wide, deep trenches through the hills to connect them all. But building the canal in Panama involved a deeper challenge.

A *political* one.

Given the geography, the only logical countries in which to situate the canal were Nicaragua, and the Panamanian region of Colombia. (Panama was not yet an independent country, and that's an important piece of this story.) Neither of these small nations had the money nor the engineering expertise to attempt what would surely be one of the biggest construction projects the world had ever seen.

It would take a much bigger and richer country to build such a canal. The project needed a nation—France, Germany, Great Britain, the Netherlands or the United States—with extensive, technical engineering experience, and the financial resources that could be brought to bear. But Nicaragua and Colombia were sovereign countries, and even a rich nation cannot build on another's land without a treaty in place.

There were other issues that needed equitable resolution. Which country would operate the canal? Who would receive the money from the ships passing through? Who would protect the canal in times of war?

The construction project, once started, would be the most expensive ever undertaken. Only a country with deep pockets, tremendous patience and a long-term vision could consider it, for the canal could easily take a full decade to build, exceeding the terms of any United States president or European head of state.

But the world was an optimistic place in the 1870s and 1880s. Technology was advancing—steam power had come into its own and railroads (thanks to Brunel and others) were now commonplace. The transatlantic telegraph cable had been successfully laid across the ocean floor, enabling near instant intercontinental communication for the first time (more on this in a later chapter). The telephone was invented in 1876; electric lights were installed in parts of Manhattan in 1882; the first automobile was built in 1885. Confidence was high, and there was every reason to believe that the technology would continue to advance to meet every new challenge that arose.

Politically, however, this era was complex.

The United States had still not recovered from the trauma of civil war. A newly unified Germany was gaining strength in Europe. The British Empire was at the height of its power. France's excellent educational facilities were turning out the greatest engineers of that time.[12] The French diplomat Ferdinand de Lesseps had just brought the ten-year project to build the sea-level Suez Canal to a successful conclusion, connecting the Red Sea to the Mediterranean, and through them the Atlantic and Indian Oceans.

Now the time had come to dig another such canal, connecting the Atlantic and Pacific Oceans. Whichever nation built and operated it would become a global leader, through military prowess and improved trade. It would take a master of diplomacy and political foresight to complete the canal. Into this mix stepped a fascinating cast of characters, but only one would emerge as the person who could achieve the greatest *politically driven* engineering feat the world had ever seen: Theodore Roosevelt.

The challenges facing Roosevelt and others who desired a canal were many, and none were easily solved. The two biggest challenges were exactly where to build it, and what exactly would be built.

Roosevelt did not always make perfect decisions. While he was quick to correct wrong ones, political opponents and the press decried his methods. The size and scale of the canal, and how it would be built, is a story of decisiveness and determination ranking among the most astonishing undertakings of all time. It is not embellishment to put its greatness on the same pedestal as Stonehenge, the Pyramids and the Great Wall of China.

But, as you will see, the Panama Canal is something altogether quite different.

One of the biggest decisions: Nicaragua or Panama?

The Panamanian region of Colombia as a potential route created many liabilities. It was filled with thick jungles, swamps, and rainforests, teeming with poisonous snakes and dangerous insects. Fatal and debilitating diseases were rife, including yellow fever, malaria and dysentery. The rainy season lasted eight to nine months of the year. Floods, landslides and long bouts of inclement weather, with high humidity and temperatures reaching 120 °F (49 °C), could quickly hamper progress. At times the climate was so damp that it rusted metal equipment quickly, clothing and shoes would never dry out and leather goods would go moldy. Its Chagres River—one of the most volatile rivers in the world—flooded regularly, rising as much as 40 feet (12 m) in a single rainstorm.

Even with all this, Panama did have some appealing attributes.

In the 1850s, the United States had gained experience there through their build of the first interoceanic railroad, stretching from Colón on the Atlantic side to Panama City on the Pacific side. The railroad's right-of-way seemed like the logical route for a canal

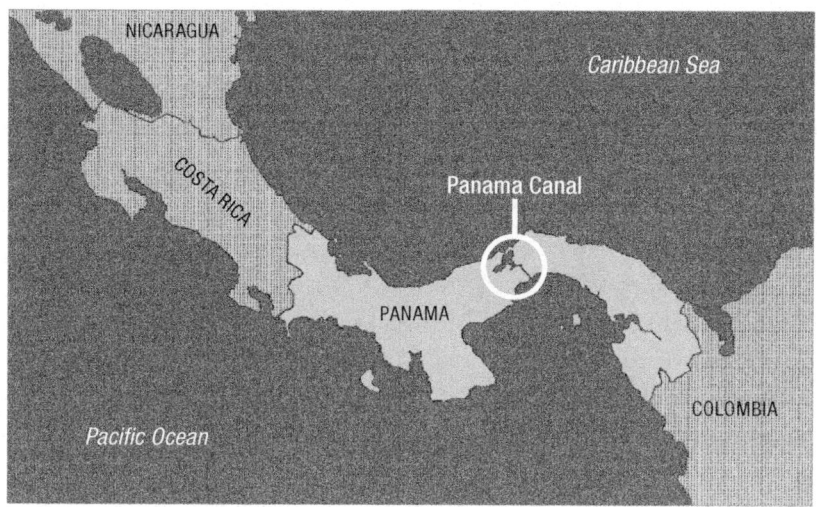

Central America showing the location of the Panama Canal..

to follow as well, but hard lessons were learned from that railroad's construction. Any country attempting to build in Panama would need to take them into consideration—that railroad project took five years to build compared to the original two-year estimate, and cost six times the original budget.

Nicaragua, meanwhile, offered a more pleasant climate, a friendly government, 100 miles (160 km) of navigable water on Lake Nicaragua, and its own low pass through the Continental Divide. But it, too, had drawbacks. It would need two artificial harbors to be built; Panama would need only one. Any canal across Nicaragua would need to follow a more curved route, tripling the transit time for a ship sailing from the Pacific to the Atlantic. And it had another serious geological problem.

Volcanoes.

The country's pride in them was clear—they were depicted on postage stamps and the national coat of arms, but volcanic eruptions were frequent and risked damaging canal construction and operations.

Roosevelt preferred Nicaragua.

Another big decision: A sea-level canal or locks?

Panama appealed in another way: it offered a possible sea-level canal route without the need for locks.

In theory, digging deep enough would enable a ship to sail from the Pacific to the Atlantic in one continuous movement. Nicaragua would definitely have required a lock-based canal to raise a ship up from one ocean to the level of Lake Nicaragua and, after sailing across, lower it back down through another set of locks, to the sea level of the other ocean.

A canal with no locks—the way the Suez Canal was built—would have significant advantages. It was thought to be a faster build because there would be no moving parts, making it cheaper and easier to maintain. Plus, sailings through a canal matching the level of the sea would be quicker. With ships being built longer, wider and with more displacement volume, one question was: how big would the locks actually need to be?

Everyone who looked seriously at the challenge—with the exception of one person who lived before Roosevelt's time—favored a sea-level canal.

De Lesseps versus de Lépinay

Ferdinand de Lesseps was no engineer, but he was a dynamic individual who received tremendous acclaim for his work on the Suez Canal. At a conference in Paris in 1879, representatives from around the world debated how to build an interoceanic canal in Latin America. De Lesseps favored a sea-level canal through Panama; the Americans at the conference favored Nicaragua. (Theodore Roosevelt was not at the conference. In 1879, he was still obtaining his undergraduate education at Harvard. His career in politics would begin many years later.)

De Lesseps argued that with the Panama route being half the length of the Suez Canal, it could be built twice as fast.

The only dissenter was a French engineer named Adolphe Godin de Lépinay. Unlike others at the conference, he had real experience building in Latin America—in his case a railway—so understood the complexity of its terrain and climate. (Railways would prove to be surprisingly important to building the canal.)

De Lépinay presented a different plan.

His idea was a lock-based canal across Panama that included building two dams to create two artificial lakes, both situated approximately 85 feet (26 m) above sea level. One of the rivers to be dammed and controlled was the turbulent Chagres River.

The dams would flood enough of the interior land, so that the shores of the artificial lakes would be as close to each ocean as possible, but those shores would still be 85 feet above the ocean. Canal locks would be needed to bring ships up to the level of the lake water and then back down on the other side.

This was easier said than done.

It would require building the largest dam in the world to control the volatile Chagres, which in turn would create the largest artificial lake in the world.

De Lépinay's plan had many advantages. With the Chagres under control the risk of flooding from the river would be eliminated, its water would feed the locks and the wide lake would enable ships to cross faster. Equally important, the dig through the Continental Divide, at the location called Culebra Cut, could be shallower since it could stay above sea level, rather than significantly below it. Other digging could also be minimized, saving time, money, and workers' lives.

His plan required a number of locks, and by the 1880s lock construction was well understood. Canal locks had been built over the centuries around the world. The brilliance of de Lépinay's approach was that it handed Panama one of Nicaragua's advantages: ships could sail across the majority of the country via one large lake.

Despite these obvious benefits de Lépinay's plan was ignored. The project was handed to seventy-four-year-old De Lesseps, who gained backing for his sea-level canal and attracted individual investors to fund it.

Work began in 1881.

Underestimating the challenge—the French attempt

The French attempt ran into difficulties from the start. Panama was not the Suez. It was a more complex and hazardous environment. Rather than staying close to the construction, De Lesseps remained in Paris, and made decisions from there. He steadfastly refused to change his desire for a sea-level canal until it was too late.

Under de Lesseps, the French invested heavily, sending giant steam shovels, dynamite, tools and supplies, locomotives and railroad cars, and other equipment to Panama. They built worker villages with dormitories, stores, and state-of-the-art tropical medicine hospitals. They hired engineers and recruited thousands of workers. Digging began in earnest after clearing a swath of jungle along the route.

However, de Lesseps and his team underestimated everything. The jungle was far more deadly than imagined. Yellow fever and malaria claimed so many lives that, at times, sixty- to seventy-five percent of the people arriving to work fell ill, and died, within a few months of setting foot in Panama.

At one end, the Chagres River flooded regularly, hampering progress and damaging works. At the other end, digging the Culebra Cut, an artificial valley the French would create through the mountainous Continental Divide, proved to be a near impossible task. 330 vertical feet (100 m) of rock and clay would have to be dug through. The dig would not only have to slice through the tops of these not very tall mountains, it would have to reach 30 feet (9 m) below sea level, along one continuous 9 mile (14 km) stretch.

These dimensions may not seem all that daunting, until you consider the bottom width of the canal would need to be 300 feet (91 m) wide, and the sides would need to slope away to prevent mudslides, meaning the top width would have to be at least 600 feet (183 m) wide. The best equipment of the day was not up to the task.

The geological underpinning at Culebra was a mix of earth, rock, and clay which absorbed and concentrated the heavy local rainfall. Months of successful work digging in this region could be lost in a single landslide. There was no physical way to shore up the sides of the Cut. With engineers and personnel dying in their hundreds from tropical disease, there was a clear lack of leadership. Adding to these hardships was a Colombian civil war (Panama was still part of Colombia), an earthquake, and racial unrest among the workers.

Partway through the construction process, de Lesseps hired the engineer Philippe Bunau-Varilla, who rose up the ranks within a single year to oversee the project. At the age of twenty-seven, he was in charge of 19,000 workers and the greatest engineering endeavor the modern world had ever seen.

Faced with rising costs and slow progress, talk of failure circulated. De Lesseps' plan for a sea-level canal was unravelling.

In 1887 De Lesseps relented, and agreed to build a lock-based canal. He hired Gustave Eiffel, who had just finished designing the Eiffel Tower—destined to become the tallest structure in the world at that time—to plan the locks, dams and other apparatus.

But the locks were never built.

Within two years the Canal Company, having sold more shares on the basis of unfounded optimism, went bankrupt. The cost was appalling.

It turned into one of the greatest financial scandals in history, in which 800,000 French people lost their investments—for some, this was their life savings. De Lesseps and Eiffel were charged with fraud and mismanagement.

After eight years, the French effort resulted in 20,000 dead or dying workers, and a loss of 1.4 billion French francs, all in the effort of excavating 65,000,000 cubic yards (50,000,000 cubic meters) of earth, only one-sixth of the amount ultimately needed to create a viable canal.

The French gave up in 1889, and no other nation took up the challenge.

It was into this mess that the United States stepped carefully—under the artful leadership of Theodore Roosevelt.

Chapter 12
Competing Visions For The Canal

The French had envisioned a canal that would speed up trade. Roosevelt had something entirely different in mind.

A naval historian from his early days when he wrote *The Naval War of 1812*, he believed that a strong Navy was a sign of a nation's military might. The United States was a two-ocean country. A canal in Panama would enable the ships of her Navy to reach either shore easily in times of war or peace. Such a canal would push an emerging America into a position of world leadership, with a military presence that could command all the seas and usurp Europe's long-held dominance.

Years after the failed French attempt, while Roosevelt was serving as governor of New York State and McKinley was serving his first term as president, a treaty was negotiated in 1900 between the United States and Great Britain, giving rights to the US to build the canal.

Roosevelt, who was at the time "merely" a governor of one of the forty-five US states (Oklahoma, New Mexico, Arizona, Alaska and Hawaii did not become states until later), immediately saw problems with the treaty. Although some said it was not a governor's role to interfere, Roosevelt charged into the national limelight by claiming that the treaty was misguided. It allowed for the canal to be built but did not authorize the United States to protect it with military fortifications. Roosevelt's interference sent the treaty back to the drawing board.

Within a matter of months, Roosevelt became McKinley's running mate for his second term, and in March 1901, Roosevelt was sworn in as the Vice President of the United States. After McKinley's assassination, he became President.

Now that Roosevelt was the nation's leader, he wasted no time in putting his own vision for the canal into reality. In his very first address to Congress (the same one in which he also described his vision for conservation in the United States), Roosevelt described the need for a US-built and US-owned interoceanic canal, detailing with great enthusiasm the military and trade advantages it would inevitably bring.

The military advantage of moving warships quickly from one coast to the other was obvious. During the recent Spanish–American War when the greatest US warship was on the west coast but was needed in Cuba, an interminable two-month wait followed while the ship sailed around Cape Horn below South America.

The canal would also vastly improve trade between the east coast of the United States and Asia, and between the US west coast and Europe. And it would add one more valuable advantage to the fast-growing United States: the ability to ship goods from one US coast to the other without going around the bottom of South America at Cape Horn. Also at play was the idea that US engineering, hard work and ingenuity would succeed where the French had tried and failed.

In December 1901, the Hay–Pauncefote Treaty between the United States and Great Britain, giving the go-ahead for the canal, was signed into law by Roosevelt and the British. Even better, it included permission for Roosevelt's fortifications to protect it. With the French effort over, and de Lesseps and Eiffel barely avoiding imprisonment for their misdeeds, Philippe Bunau-Varilla became the agent designated to sell the French canal assets in Panama to the highest bidder. Bunau-Varilla sought $109 million dollars for the French assets and the rights to dig the site.

While Roosevelt and the United States still preferred the Nicaragua route, and had minimal interest in the failed French dig and all its rusting equipment, a Nicaraguan volcanic eruption in 1902—during the Senate debate—swung the vote 42 to 34 in favor of a sea-level route through Panama.

Roosevelt accepted the decision.

A bloodless revolution—well, nearly

If the United States was going to build in Panama, it wanted to secure the rights to control a ten-mile-wide swath of land along the route, cutting across the isthmus. But at the time Panama was still part of Colombia, and their constitution did not allow giving away pieces of their land to other nations.

This did not daunt Roosevelt.

Using all the cunning he'd honed during his years as a cowboy, politician and head of the Rough Riders (the cavalry unit that fought fearlessly in the Spanish-American War), Roosevelt sent spies to see if there was a way to achieve what he wanted. Receiving reports back that Colombia would not negotiate a reasonable price he set about backing the Panamanian nationalists seeking their independence from Colombia. The goal was to stage a quiet Panamanian revolution. Roosevelt wanted to ensure it would end quickly, peacefully, and without bloodshed.

Revolution day was set for November 3, 1903.

The Panamanian nationalists were supported by the presence of a US naval warship. Colombian soldiers who arrived on the scene were paid with cash to leave without fighting. Colombia gave in. Within a few days, Roosevelt's administration announced its recognition of Panama as an independent country.

The one-time chief engineer and sales agent for the failed French effort, Philippe Bunau-Varilla, was a wily character, and was now working on his own. Arriving in Washington ahead of the now-independent Panamanian delegation, he falsely claimed to be an official Panamanian representative and quickly negotiated a treaty with the US Secretary of State, John Hay.

The United States would get what it wanted—a perpetual lease on a ten-mile-wide, fifty-mile-long strip of land (16 km by 80 km), stretching across the new nation of Panama, that would become the sovereign domain of the United States government—in exchange for a ten million dollar fee paid to Panama. In a separate transaction, also devised by Bunau-Varilla, the United States paid forty million dollars in 1904 to purchase the French infrastructure and equipment.

This was the largest real estate deal in the history of the world at the time.

Roosevelt had engineered a tenuous diplomatic solution in a situation that, had it gone wrong, would have resulted in a lengthy and bloody Colombian civil war. In the end, Panama achieved independence; America gained a partially dug Canal Zone; money exchanged hands. The casualties on the day of the revolution were a shopkeeper and a donkey—both tragically in the wrong place at the wrong time.

Roosevelt took a beating in the press and from some politicians for his audacious actions. He was accused of being imperialist, and of undermining the reputation of the United States by having the arrogance to fund a revolution in a sovereign country. But he had achieved his objective: the right to build an interoceanic canal, totally under the control of the United States.

The people could argue about Roosevelt and his tactics all they wanted, he felt, but meanwhile canal construction would be under way.

It was only weeks later that the Panamanians learned that Bunau-Varilla had given away such a wide strip of land with complete sovereign rights to the United States, literally dividing their newly formed country in two. They were expecting a narrower, six-mile-wide Canal Zone (9.6 km) and certainly not one totally under American control.

"Make the dirt fly"

Roosevelt wanted swift action. He placed the engineer, John Finley Wallace, in charge and appointed a seven-person Isthmian Canal Commission (ICC) to oversee and approve all expenditures. May 4, 1904 would be the official United States start date. Wallace wisely wanted a year to assess the situation but Roosevelt's instruction was, "Make the dirt fly."

The United States, under Roosevelt, was headed down the exact same disastrous approach the French had taken: building a sea-level canal. Jungle overgrowth, uncleared mudslides, as well as rusted and damaged French equipment and infrastructure meant that the United States team was not starting with the advantage they might have hoped.

Every mistake the French had already made was being recreated in the Canal Zone. The United States installed enormous steam shovels that could dig up eight tons of rubble at once and place it on a train car, but it soon became clear that the spoil could not be transported away quickly or efficiently.

Yellow fever, malaria and dysentery were still wreaking havoc on the many-thousand-person workforce. Like the French, the United States sent engineers from the home country (white men) to design the canal and oversee workers from the Caribbean and elsewhere (mostly but not entirely black men). With disease running rampant in the early months, United States personnel left the project in droves. By mid 1905, sixty- to seventy-five percent of United States staff had left, resigned or died. The French disaster was being repeated by the United States.

After one year the United States effort had embarrassingly not even come close to matching the volume of dirt the French excavated. At this rate, to complete the dig of a sea-level canal could take twenty-seven years.

As well as a man of action Roosevelt was also a quick learner, and not shy about admitting he'd made a mistake. When his chief engineer Wallace resigned from the project, Roosevelt faced tough decisions.

Waging a different kind of war

At the start of the United States effort, Colonel William Gorgas, a medical doctor, was appointed as Chief Sanitary Engineer in Panama. Dr. Gorgas had years of experience in tropical medicine, having spent part of his career in Cuba, where doctors knew for certain that mosquitoes were the cause of yellow fever. However, this was not a popular belief in the United States. There, doctors, politicians, and everyone else, thought that yellow fever was due to poor sanitation.

Gorgas had successfully eradicated mosquitoes in Havana before coming to the Canal Zone in 1904. Thinking he could have the same success in Panama he drafted a plan that would cost $1,000,000—the most expensive and largest public health initiative ever proposed anywhere in the world.

The ICC (Isthmian Canal Commission), believing that yellow fever was due to "bad air," only approved $50,000. Dr. Gorgas lobbied for the full amount. The ICC fought back and sought to replace him. Word reached Roosevelt, who consulted with a medical expert he trusted—his personal physician—who told him point-blank: if you want your canal you must fully fund Gorgas' plan.

So Roosevelt did.

Enter John Stevens

With Wallace out, Roosevelt made another prophetically wise decision. He appointed John Stevens as Chief Engineer, giving him the enormous task of rescuing the largest construction project on the planet. Stevens had built the Great Northern Railroad across the United States. He was cut from the same cloth as Isambard Kingdom Brunel; he knew every mile of track of his railroad because he had surveyed the land himself.

Stevens came into the Canal Zone and, despite Roosevelt's continued plea to make dirt fly, ordered work to stop. He quickly realized the problem was not the digging. The problem was the

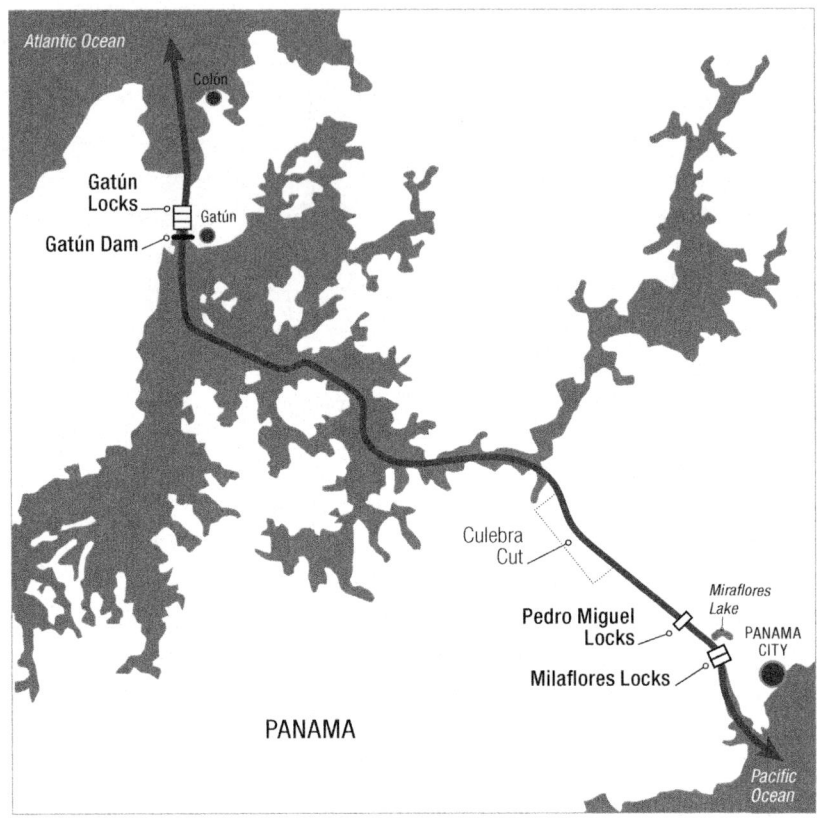

The Panama Canal.

railroad. Fixing the railroad so it could carry away debris faster, would speed up the digging. He also identified other key issues, including the need for improved workers' housing, and more nutritious food and conditions for both the American engineers and the multinational labor force.

Being a railroad engineer enabled Stevens to find solutions to laborious, time consuming and dangerous work. He had his men invent a "track shifter"—a swinging boom mounted on a flat train car that could lift and move whole segments of train tracks. With this machine, twelve men could re-lay a mile (1.6 km) of track in one day—work that would normally have taken 600 men. He replaced debris-carrying train cars with ones equipped with plows to sweep out the heavy, sticky clay and rocks. This speeded up the emptying process. A train consisting of twenty carriages could now be emptied in as little as ten minutes.

With Dr. Gorgas focusing on recruiting a 4,000-person team to eradicate every mosquito and its larvae in existence in the five-hundred-square-mile Canal Zone, including the two urban areas Colón and Panama City, Stevens concentrated on solving the engineering problems of the canal.

For the 9 mile (14 km) Culebra Cut, which had so stymied the French, Stevens chose a different approach. Reminiscent of how Brunel engineered the excavation of the Box Tunnel, Stevens started the digging at both ends simultaneously. By ingeniously laying enough parallel train track along the length of the cut through the mountains Stevens could have a locomotive pulling carriages up the Cut empty, get filled, and then descend the other side of the Cut full. Although this maximized efficiency it also made one fact very clear: no amount of engineering efficiency would overcome the sheer volume of earth needing to be removed to dig a sea-level canal.

Stevens now faced the most daunting challenge of his career: telling President Roosevelt that a sea-level canal was folly.

While Gorgas' team was inspecting every building, outhouse and shed, searching for and fixing cracks in the structures, fumigating, putting screens on all windows, clearing swamps and putting a layer of oil on every puddle of water and cistern to prevent mosquitoes from breeding, Stevens set sail for Washington DC.

Roosevelt makes another big decision

What Stevens proposed to Roosevelt and Congressional committees was exactly the plan that de Lépinay had advised the French to do in the conference of 1879: build locks, dams and artificial lakes. Armed with firsthand knowledge of Panama, Stevens now knew a lock system could be built faster, cheaper and with more assured success than the "making dirt fly" strategy.

He explained to Roosevelt that unless the Chagres River was tamed by a dam it would keep flooding the canal works. Even if a sea-level canal could be built, it would only be operable half of the year. The downside of a lock-based approach was that over fifty percent of the excavation done by the French in the 1880s, for which the United States had paid such a high price to Bunau-Varilla, would now be useless. It would become flooded after the Gatun Dam was built across the Chagres.

Here again, Roosevelt was quick to follow the advice of the best minds in the business. He quickly agreed with Stevens. This single decision changed the course of maritime and world history.

By mid-1906, Dr. Gorgas' magic was working. Yellow fever cases and deaths were diminishing. By November of that year, Dr. Gorgas called some of his assistants into a room at the main hospital. He told them to look carefully at the deceased person being examined because that individual would be the last ever yellow fever death in the Canal Zone.

Theodore Roosevelt's funding of the doctor's initiative, and Gorgas' ability to execute it in the swamp and jungle rainforest of Panama, is as remarkable as the canal itself. Every single mosquito in the five-hundred-square-mile Canal Zone had been killed.

Roosevelt's photo shoot at the Culebra Cut

Roosevelt decided to travel to Panama to see the work firsthand. Even in his earliest days as a politician he was not one to follow procedure, and this trip would be a major break in protocol. It would be the first time a sitting US president had traveled outside the country. This was an important milestone, both for the morale of the workers as well as for the media. The world was fascinated by Roosevelt, although some of the media proclaimed that the president leaving United States soil violated 100 years of American tradition.

In typical Roosevelt fashion, he wanted to see Panama at its worst. So he scheduled the trip for November 1906—the height of the rainy season. (Like Brunel and Amundsen, Roosevelt enjoyed getting his hands dirty.) Although parades, speeches and events were planned for his arrival by ship, Roosevelt left the ship one day early to see firsthand, the unglamorized Canal Zone's towns, hospitals and living quarters.

During his visit, Roosevelt took charge of his own schedule. To everyone's surprise, he even ate lunch with the workers in their dining area on one of the days. He talked with the white engineers and the black workers, seeking a broad and unvarnished view of the entire construction project. Roosevelt wanted to form his own impressions.

On the official days, he gave speeches praising the work, and talked about its importance both for the United States and the world. In the pouring rain, he visited the Culebra Cut. Wearing his white suit and white hat, he climbed aboard one of the great hulking digging machines and sat in the driver's seat, receiving instructions on how to operate it.

This was America at its grandest.

Roosevelt was media-savvy, and here he was in the dirty grime of the largest construction site the modern world had ever seen, in a pristine white suit, exhibiting daring leadership and showcasing American power. It may have been one of the greatest black-and-white photographic moments of the decade, and one of the most memorable photographs ever taken of a United States president. Up until that point, US presidents were either painted, or photographed, in a statesman- or businessman-like pose.

The unspoken message was: the United States would succeed where France, representing old-world Europe, had failed.

His visit marked the turning point in the canal's progress.

Roosevelt makes another inspired hiring decision

Chief Engineer Stevens resigned two and a half months after Roosevelt's visit, explaining in a long letter to the president he had no desire to continue because the canal was only "a big ditch."

Roosevelt did not like quitters, but he knew that Stevens was the key to what the United States had achieved so far. Roosevelt replaced him with George Washington Goethals, a civil engineer from the US Army Corps of Engineers.

Goethals was a superb choice given all the large construction work still to be done. The world's largest dam at Gatun still had to be built, which in turn would create the world's largest artificial lake; next would be the twelve massive locks (six on the Pacific side and six on the Atlantic side); and finally the completion of the Culebra Cut with its never-ending mudslides and setbacks. The tasks definitely required a different skill set than Stevens had.

Goethals dealt with all this during his seven years on the project, which continued well past the end of Roosevelt's presidency in March 1909. By May 1913, the digging in the Culebra Cut was finished. By August 1913, the locks of the canal could finally be filled with water, and with great fanfare in October of that year, the Culebra Cut was also filled with water. The official opening of the Panama Canal happened on August 15, 1914, eleven days after the start of World War I.

Theodore Roosevelt did not visit the Canal Zone again, and never saw the finished canal.

He was still very much alive in 1914, but he was busy exploring the world on one of his many post-presidential adventures (described in Chapter 22).

As for the canal, it remains to this day one of the most important structures ever built. How important? The next chapter defines its legacy.

Chapter 13

The Monumental Legacy Of The Panama Canal

The Panama Canal would sit comfortably in a top list of amazing structures dating back to the dawn of humankind, including Stonehenge, the Pyramids, the Great Wall of China, the Taj Mahal and others. However, there is one singular thing that sets the Panama Canal apart from all these. Those structures are static. Once built, they do not move.

The Panama Canal is more than a structure. As historians and authors like David McCullough have pointed out, the Panama Canal was the world's greatest machine at the time of its building. The many moving parts—some mechanical and some water powered—are in constant motion. Enormous sets of gates in each of the twelve locks must move in a coordinated and timely fashion whenever a ship approaches. By 2010, just under a century since it was first opened, over one million ships had traversed the canal.

The canal's design ensured that each lock could easily accommodate the largest ship ever built in that era, which included ones that were larger than the *Titanic*. To give you an idea of the magnitude, each individual lock is 100 feet (30 m) wide and 1,000 feet (300 m) long, over three times larger than any lock previously built anywhere in the world. If just one Panama Canal lock was stood on end, it would be taller than the Eiffel Tower, the tallest structure in the world at the time of the Canal's construction.

In today's world—and this may be hard to believe—one lock stood on its end would be the 27th tallest building in the United States. Except in the case of the canal, twelve of these giant locks were built, and they were built over 100 years ago.[13]

Although concrete had been around since the Roman Empire, it had never been used in this quantity, and never before had been used in structures expected to last for decades or centuries while half, or fully, submerged every day, with millions of gallons of water flowing in and out of them, almost on an hourly basis. All of the large concrete dams and structures built since then owe their lineage to the successful use of this material in Panama.

The canal's design is ingenious. In an era where there was no computer modeling, and no way to run tests at even a smaller scale, the entire canal had to be precision built. But no one would know if it really worked, until it was filled with water from end to end.

Water flows downhill into the locks from the two large, artificial lakes that were created as part of the project. At the time of building, Lake Gatun was the largest artificial lake in the world, created by the Gatun Dam, the largest dam in the world.

To enable the transit of one ship through the canal, a staggering 52 million gallons (236 million liters) of fresh water passes from the lakes into the locks, and then into the ocean. Even with the flow of this much water, a single lock in the Panama Canal can fill in fifteen minutes. All electricity required for the canal is generated by the Gatun Dam, and it was built and delivering electrical power at a time when household electricity connection in the United States was still in its infancy.

The Panama Canal today allows thirty-five to forty ships to pass daily from one ocean to the other.[14] Trains remain a vital part of the canal. Ships are pulled through the locks by specially constructed locomotives—the first of their kind. Goods that we use every day—cars, computers, furniture, food, clothing—all pass through the Panama Canal.

If you consider it for what it is, a great machine, the Panama Canal may only have been surpassed in the last one-hundred years by the invention of the ENIAC (the first large-scale, programmable computer, built in 1946), and the International Space Station.

However, in *their* construction one did not have to battle swamps, jungles, the constant threat of destructive and deadly mudslides, nine-month rainy seasons, 120 °F (49 °C) heat, ninety-eight-percent humidity, and rampant and deadly yellow fever (solved by the greatest public health initiative ever undertaken up to that time). And, ensure the removal of enough earth to create the equivalent of —and this, too, may be hard to believe—a Great Wall of China if it ran from Newfoundland, Canada right down to the Florida Keys.[15]

The dream of joining the oceans that began in the 1500s finally became a reality. It required the combined efforts of thousands of hard working people backed by the decision-making power, political prowess, vision and determination of a uniquely talented statesman: Theodore Roosevelt.

The canal transformed the globe. With its completion America delivered what Theodore Roosevelt promised: The United States became a world superpower, ready to grab the mantle from the old world.

Lessons in leadership taught by the building of the Panama Canal

- **Hire people who think strategically and act tactically.** John Stevens, Dr. Gorgas and George Goethals were leaders with both strategic vision and a detailed, tactical understanding of the tasks required to complete the work. People with both talents in equal measure are rare. In the Canal Zone, they made excellent leaders because they gained the respect of people at all levels in the hierarchy.

- **Listen to your team when they speak.** The engineer, John Stevens and Dr. Gorgas both told Roosevelt exactly what needed to be said. In modern political parlance it's called, talking truth to power.

"Make the dirt fly" may have been a great political slogan, but Stevens insisted that a year spent assessing the situation would be of far greater benefit than a year of action with no plan. Dr. Gorgas fought back when his plan to kill every single mosquito in the Canal Zone didn't receive the funding it needed. Once Roosevelt decided to back Gorgas, he backed him fully.

What we can take away from this is that by only enacting partial measures, we might actually hinder a project's success. For example, had Roosevelt only committed half the funds Dr. Gorgas requested, the yellow fever eradication program would have been a resounding failure, because to kill only half of the mosquitoes in the Canal Zone would have meant the problem still existed.

Leaders who can listen and learn will be far more successful than those who don't. It is far better to make informed corrections based on solid knowledge provided by your team, than to believe all is fine when it may not be.

- **The real problem isn't always the obvious one.** This might be one of the most important lessons in this book. As Stevens rightly pointed out to Roosevelt, digging the Culebra Cut was not a digging problem but a railroad one. To achieve greater success on any project, it's best to take time to identify the main, underlying problem that might be hampering progress.

- **Admit when you have made a mistake.** De Lesseps refused to accept that a sea-level canal was impossible until it was too late. Roosevelt headed down exactly the same path. The difference was that after Stevens explained to Roosevelt why a canal with locks, dams and artificial lakes would be better, Roosevelt agreed to the change. It's not easy to admit when we're wrong and to change the trajectory of a project midway, but Roosevelt proved it could be done in a high-profile, high-risk venture like the Panama Canal.

- **Look after your people.** Roosevelt's longstanding respect for ordinary workers led to better protections for them during the highly dangerous canal work. His on-site leaders, Wallace, Stevens, Dr. Gorgas and Goethals, made continual improvements to the workers' conditions. They eradicated disease, improved living quarters and food, and tried (but not always successfully) to ensure worker safety.

There is one more lesson to be gleaned from this: had de Lesseps focused on building de Lépinay's plan for a lock-based canal rather than dismissing it out of hand, the French could have been successful. In that case, this book would have been about an Explorer (Amundsen), an Engineer (Brunel) and a Diplomat (de Lesseps), for de Lesseps would have been responsible for building the two greatest artificial waterways in the world: the Suez and Panama Canals.

Visiting the Panama Canal today

There are short boat tours that take visitors through a few locks, or longer ones that complete the full ocean-to-ocean transit up through the locks at one side, crossing Lake Gatun and the Culebra Cut (renamed as the Gaillard Cut) and descending through the locks on the other side. Alternatively, there are international cruise ships that include the interoceanic passage as part of their itinerary.

The Miraflores Visitor Center, near Panama City, is both a museum and place to watch large ships passing through the locks. In the city you can also find the Panama Canal Museum. On the Colón side, you can visit the Gatun locks.

Another way to see the Canal Zone is to travel on the Panama Canal Railway. The best months to visit are January through March, but if you really want to experience Panama the way Theodore Roosevelt did, then be sure to visit in the height of the rainy season.

The first official ship through the Panama Canal was the SS *Ancon*, but before that a much more famous ship was invited to be the first. That ship was the greatest polar vessel ever built: the *Fram*.

Due to necessary repairs to the ship and still unfinished work on the canal the timing for such a symbolic event did not align. We can only imagine how memorable a sight it would have been to see the iconic, wooden, three-masted *Fram*, captained by the explorer Roald Amundsen, making the first ocean-to-ocean crossing through the most magnificent waterway ever built.

Roald Amundsen was no ordinary polar explorer. His expedition teams, quite literally, followed him to the ends of the Earth. Our next chapters unveil the decisions he made in pursuing his bold achievements that helped map and define the very end points of our planet.

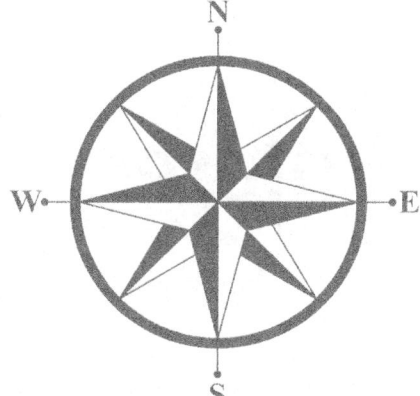

Part Three

Let No Obstacle Turn You Back: Roald Amundsen

The Explorer

"At best the climate in Antarctica is about the worst in the world"

—*Roald Amundsen*

Chapter 14
The Open Window

The frigid, Norwegian winter air swept through young Roald Amundsen's open bedroom window. What better way to prepare for the life of a polar explorer than to sleep night after night like this?

Growing up in the late 1800s meant living in a world where more was known about the moon than the ends of the Earth. The size, mass and rotational path of the moon had long been calculated, and its features had been examined (by telescope), mapped and given Latin names.

In stark contrast, the polar regions of our own planet were largely unmapped, their mysteries beyond the fringes of the sea still shrouded in mist and ice, quietly enticing those with a desire for deeper discovery.

For anyone dreaming of exploration in Amundsen's day, three enticing land and sea-based challenges still beckoned:

- **The Northwest Passage**—A sea route sought since the 1500s, connecting the Atlantic Ocean to the Pacific across the top of Canada. If found, it had the potential to speed up trade between Europe and Asia. Many lives had already been lost in the centuries-long search for the elusive, icy route.

- **The North Pole**—Serious attempts to reach it began around 1820 (roughly coinciding with the design of the Thames Tunnel described in Chapter 1). At that time, no one even knew if there was an open sea, ice-covered sea or even land at the North Pole.

- **The South Pole**—An even more elusive destination, since Antarctica had only just been discovered. No one would set foot on the Antarctic continent until 1895.

It would take an extraordinary individual to achieve one of these three geographical prizes. To do so would secure their name among the world's greatest explorers.

Roald Amundsen was determined to be a contender.

Already captivated with the spirit of an extreme adventurer, young Amundsen knew that he needed to become conditioned for a life in the polar regions. Bracing himself against the frigid Norwegian winter air to acclimate, he must have pondered questions like: *What traits make a successful explorer? Why do some polar expeditions succeed, and others fail?*

Once he had decided on his life's passion, Amundsen dropped out of medical school and immersed himself in the tragic stories of the previous explorers who'd attempted to find the Northwest Passage. He reasoned there had to be better ways to explore these regions other than by the methods of those who'd previously tried—efforts that had ended in hardship, and sometimes death, for so many.

Amundsen spent a lifetime learning from others, striving for achievement, and inventing—dare we say engineering—new ways to improve expedition travel.

Just like Isambard Kingdom Brunel and Theodore Roosevelt, Amundsen's ambitions were bold. And just like these other two trailblazers, his achievements were equally breathtaking, and even more dangerous.

"Victory awaits him who has everything in order—luck, people call it."

—*Roald Amundsen*

Iceberg, similar to those seen in the Northwest Passage.

Chapter 15
Adventure Is Just Bad Planning

The 500-Year Quest For A Northwest Passage

To fully understand Roald Amundsen's life as a polar explorer you really have to imagine a world where vast, unexplored regions on Earth still existed. Those empty spaces on the map and on the globe, held great intrigue—a romantic essence if you will—and called to those with adventurous spirit to be the first to set foot upon them.

Like all romantic notions, this was only a hazy, filtered dream—a fantasy out of touch with the reality of how difficult, or even tragic it would be for those attempting to conquer the unknown. But the desire to try had sent countless expeditions down paths of untold suffering and failure in the quest to find the elusive Northwest Passage.

Since the late 1400s, Europeans had speculated that a sea route existed across the top of North America that could connect Europe with Asia. Exploration at that time had led to developing European markets for Asian goods and spices. There was considerable money to be made in that commerce.

While the Panama Canal remained but a dream unrealized, a faster northern commercial route between continents would mean power, control and wealth for kings, queens, countries and trading

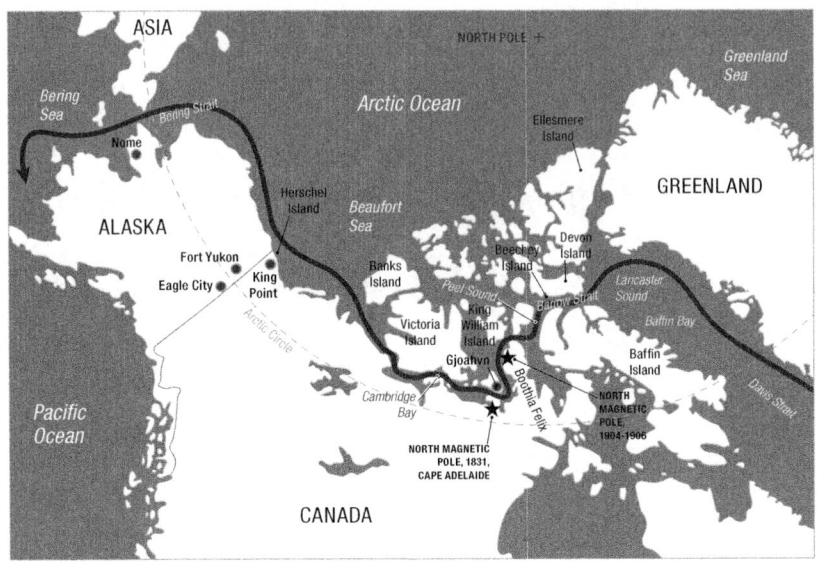

Map of the Northwest Passage as eventually sailed by Amundsen

companies. The supposed route acquired a name: the Northwest Passage. A northeast passage above Russia would also serve to connect the markets, if it could likewise be successfully navigated. Famous and experienced sea captains and explorers searched for both, but the complex of straits, shoals, islands, and especially impenetrable ice, continually intrigued and baffled them, and thwarted their efforts.

To navigators of the era, the northwest seemed the most likely route. In 1497, long before the full extent of North America came to be understood, it seemed a simple task for England's John Cabot to find a passage around the continent that Columbus had "discovered" a mere five years earlier. He failed, as did his son Sebastian, and later on Martin Frobisher, John Davis, Jacques Cartier, and a host of other European explorers. Henry Hudson died there in the 1600s, during his fourth such fruitless voyage of discovery.

A trade route to the Orient was so desirable that in 1744, the British Parliament offered a sizeable monetary reward to the first sailor who could identify one—when converted to modern currency it was more than five times the award for a Nobel Prize today. By the time the Napoleonic wars drew to a close in 1805 the reward was still unclaimed. The British Navy, built up to fight those wars, was now underemployed and to keep the men, officers, and ships busy sent some of them out find it. An expedition led by Sir John Ross was forced to turn back when it could not find a way through. John Franklin, an accomplished explorer, also tried and failed.

Just as *The Boy Hunters* inspired Theodore Roosevelt to learn more about the American west, Roald Amundsen was enraptured by the books about John Franklin's 1819 and 1823 overland explorations across the Canadian tundra. Many years before Amundsen was even born, Franklin's party had ventured into the wild with only the vaguest notion of what they might encounter there.

Franklin's goal was to find, explore and chart the coastline where the North American continent met the Arctic Ocean. Ill-equipped beyond measure in experience, adaptability and preparation, more than a few explorers never made it back. Others returned home with dreadful stories of bare survival, with hints of horrible tales in the frozen north.

In 1845, Franklin left England once again, this time with two well-found ships, the *Erebus* and *Terror*, to seek out the ultimate sea route of the Northwest Passage. They disappeared. One hundred and twenty-nine men were lost in that expedition, and many search parties looked for them over the next several years. Some crew members aboard rescue ships contracted scurvy; team members died; and vessels were lost or shipwrecked.

Young Amundsen could only wonder why.

Knowing the hardships of exploring in the polar ice, why didn't these men prepare adequately? Instead of learning from the past and pioneering new methods that would help them cope with the harsh conditions, why did they repeat the same old hidebound ways? And why were their accounts of great suffering and modest results so captivating to the reading public? Wouldn't it be more exciting to read about teams that actually succeeded?

When Amundsen looked for answers, and found they were not forthcoming, he set about to create his own. He recognized that an individual with the right kind of conditioning and preparation could accomplish what previous explorers and governments could not. Could he be the one to discover the Northwest Passage?

To succeed, he would need to replace his youthful idealism with a pragmatic understanding of what such a voyage would require.

What made the Northwest Passage so challenging?

The arctic and subarctic region was geographically complex—dotted with hundreds of large and small islands, and numerous possible sea routes around or between them. The ice and weather conditions changed yearly. What might have appeared to be a possible route one year could be clogged with ice in the next. A ship could get halfway through or farther, only to turn back because of impenetrable ice.

History is replete with stories of failed Northwest Passage expeditions that suffered from exposure, frostbite, scurvy, temperatures as low as -50° Fahrenheit (-45° C) and even murder. Expeditions ran out of food, lost their bearings, and were forced to travel on foot. Sometimes the men survived only by eating lichen and the leather of their shoes and clothing. Some had to resort to cannibalism.

The wooden ships they used were at risk of catching fire. In heavy fog and ice conditions, they had run aground on shoals or been gored by jagged rocks, and in other instances been beset in the ice, crushed, and sunk without hope of rescue.

The mental stress on the leaders and team members of a multi-year expedition, requiring overwintering with its bitterly cold weather and lack of sunlight, would have taken its toll on all participants. Unity and a focus on the goal became two of the many challenges to maintain.

The Northwest Passage remained unconquered.

Norway

Amundsen's Norwegian home with its cold winters, long nights and deep snowfalls gave him a profound understanding of subpolar conditions, and provided him with a foundation for the wider experiences he would soon seek.

Norway itself was moving toward its own sense of national identity after centuries as a vassal state under the control of either Denmark or Sweden (each owned it at various points). Norwegian artists, playwrights, composers, scientists, explorers, and cultural icons of all kinds were starting to make their impact on the intellectual life of Europe and the world. The most spectacular of all these, in Amundsen's eyes, was the explorer Fridtjof Nansen, who received resounding acclaim upon his return to Christiania (the original name for Oslo) for his breathtaking first crossing of the Greenland icecap in 1888.

In pursuit of their goal, Nansen and his five companions made a remarkable—or foolhardy, or perhaps even suicidal—decision. They had their ship drop them off on the *uninhabited* east coast of Greenland. The plan was to allow themselves to be marooned on that shore, with no recourse except to make the crossing to the inhabited west coast. At that point, Nansen and his team had two choices: find a safe way across the icecap with the limited supplies at hand (while trying not to fall into any crevasses or ice-canyons) or die trying.

Although they came near death more than once, the six brave, adventurous and resourceful men proved that the crossing could be achieved, and returned to their native land as heroes. Amundsen, then seventeen years old, was in the crowd on the quay in Christiania waiting for their triumphant arrival. It was their safe arrival that crystalized Amundsen's explorer ambition.

In the same way that Brunel's unpleasant train journey inspired him to transform rail travel, and the failed attempt by another nation to dig a canal through Panama motivated Roosevelt to do better, an inspired Amundsen stood on the quay that day determined that he would be the first to sail through the Northwest Passage.

The idea was planted and had taken root. While it would not immediately bear fruit, it pushed Amundsen to get as physically and psychologically fit as possible. He sought ways to endure and overcome the rigors of whatever hardships would arise in his future life as a polar explorer.

Inspired by Nansen's exploits, twenty-one-year-old Amundsen set out with a friend on his own winter expedition to cross the highlands of Western Norway, to the North Sea coast and back. Their lack of Arctic experience, insufficient equipment, and inadequate levels of fitness, along with unlucky blizzards with temperatures approaching -40° F (-40° C), came near to killing them.

But for Amundsen, it was the first of many hard-earned lessons to prepare him for his ultimate goal.

Undeterred, Amundsen sought out more experience toward the fulfillment of his ambition. After first trying unsuccessfully to sign on with a few polar expeditions, he shipped out instead in the summer of 1894 onboard a seal hunting ship (commonly called a sealer) working in the polar seas north of Norway.

Nansen's Greenland crossing had proved that a small expedition, consisting of a few highly trained individuals with clearly understood goals, could accomplish more than the weightiest of quasi-military polar expeditions with their legions of support staff. It was becoming clear to Amundsen that some of the failings of previous cold-climate expeditions had stemmed from conflicts between the expedition's leader and the captain of the expedition's ship. He reasoned that to achieve the most efficient results the leader must also be the ship's captain.

If Amundsen was to be an effective leader on his own expeditions, then he would have to attain his own captain's license. So, he set out to acquire hands-on, in-the-field experience. Knowing he would need more experience than a few months as a deckhand on a sealer, he set about earning his mariner's licenses—seaman, second mate, first mate, captain—on his brother's North Sea trading schooners.

Amundsen gained limited experience though from the mostly

coastal trade in ice-free waters, close to shore. What he really needed was genuine polar experience at sea, battling sea ice and navigating by feel through fog-shrouded waterways filled with uncharted reefs. These experiences, and the bracing exposure to the bitterest cold, would give Amundsen the chance to prove his mettle, both to himself and to the world at large.

More than he bargained for: polar experience aboard the *Belgica*

Roald Amundsen's opportunity came in the form of an Antarctic scientific expedition proposed by a novice explorer—Adrian de Gerlache—caught up in the romantic ideals of polar exploration. De Gerlache's plan was to explore the Weddell Sea, then work to the west along the still uncharted coast of the continent toward Cape Adare and leave a small wintering party ashore there. His intentions exceeded his abilities.

De Gerlache was no captain; his native country of Belgium had almost no seafaring history, and most importantly he had nowhere near enough money to buy and outfit a ship. However, his contagious enthusiasm and personal magnetism were enough to get his plans for the expedition underway. To achieve his aims, De Gerlache needed to find enough officers and crew to pay for the privilege, or come along as volunteers.

De Gerlache agreed to take Amundsen, still working toward his master's certificate, as an unpaid second mate, with the stipulations that he refresh his navigation skills and learn enough French and Flemish to be able to give orders to the polyglot crew. Amundsen plunged into his new studies with characteristic fervor, joining the *Belgica* as it set sail south in the summer of 1897.

Along the way, the *Belgica* picked up Dr. Frederick Cook who would serve as the ship's medic. Cook was another volunteer, but one with extensive polar credentials. Years before, he had accompanied the polar explorer Robert Peary, and Peary's equally famous assistant Matthew Henson, in an early attempt to explore northern Greenland to determine if it was just a big island or a land route to the North Pole.

In a historical twist relevant to this book, Peary and Henson had established their credentials as an exploration team when Peary was commissioned by the United States government in 1887 to go to Nicaragua, to find a viable route for an interoceanic canal. This was long before Theodore Roosevelt had risen to national prominence, and coincided with the time when the US preferred Nicaragua over Panama for any potential canal.

It was in staffing this Nicaragua undertaking that Peary first recruited Henson, who became his most trusted companion on their later expedition attempts to the North Pole. What makes the Peary-Henson partnership unusual is that in an era where almost every explorer was a white male, Matthew Henson was Black. Peary and Henson spent two years together searching for a viable canal route in the very warm Nicaraguan climate before turning their attention to Arctic expeditions.

Thanks to his own Arctic adventures with Peary and Henson, Dr. Cook had more polar experience than the rest of the *Belgica* crew combined. He was the only one on board who possessed practical knowledge about high-latitude, cold-weather survival. Combined with his medical knowledge and innate empathy, this made him the ideal mentor to Amundsen, now twenty-five years old and at the start of his polar career.

The first sledge journey on the Antarctic pack ice

De Gerlache was the expedition leader; Georges Lecointe was the ship's captain. The old, conflict-laden dichotomy quickly came into play.

Neither man had the leadership skills required for the task, and the crew were acutely aware of their shortcomings. They resented the poor decisions being made to push the ship ever deeper into the ice-clogged sea. After seven months at sea (in late February 1898), and only a few weeks after crossing the Antarctic Circle, the *Belgica* became unexpectedly frozen in the Southern Ocean sea ice.

Amundsen had longed for an experience like this, writing in his journal that "nothing could be better." But de Gerlache's poor planning had left the crew dreadfully short of the supplies needed to overwinter in the ice. Since the intention had been for the ship to leave a small wintering party and return to South America to wait out the rest of the winter season, then return in spring to retrieve them, there was insufficient cold weather clothing for everyone onboard. There was too little food to sustain the entire crew for their unplanned overwintering, and not even enough oil to keep the lamps lit and the darkness at bay.

The limited, preserved rations on hand would last the men one year, even though a ship trapped in the ice might not be freed for several years. The lessons proving the need for comprehensive preparation, and detailed advanced planning, to cope with the unexpected were not lost on Amundsen. As the winter wore on, scurvy settled in, and the men became disconsolate and weak. Months of endless Antarctic nights shrouded everything in darkness. De Gerlache and Lecointe, feeling death was approaching fast, wrote out their wills.

But they hadn't counted on the bravery of two men onboard.

If Amundsen had signed onto the voyage to gain experience, he was about to get far more than he bargained for. In the absence of leadership, Dr. Cook and Amundsen took control. Cook understood better than almost everyone in that era that the cure for scurvy was fresh food. He believed that eating only tinned meats and preserves would kill the men. So, he fed the sick men a diet of freshly killed seal and penguin. They hated the taste, but this fresh meat was the best medicine.

Dr. Cook's understanding of the causes of scurvy almost parallels Dr. Gorgas' insights discussed earlier in the Panama Canal chapters, where Gorgas correctly deduced that yellow fever was caused by mosquitoes. Both doctors ignored the conventional medical wisdom about treating these debilitating diseases, and reasoned out innovative, and ultimately successful approaches.

It was on the *Belgica* Expedition that Amundsen learned an important lesson about polar travel: experience and meticulous planning are essential to prevent suffering and death.

Amundsen and Cook were both accustomed to the ascetic lifestyle and physical hardship that polar exploration demanded. Undaunted by the conditions which had spun the other members of the expedition into despair, the pair spent the winter overhauling the sledging gear and working together to devise a new type of tent, conical in shape, for better resistance against the onslaughts of blizzards. As the Antarctic winter was ending and the first sunlight in months appeared, Cook and Amundsen left the ship on a camping trip, to test out their new tent design. Amundsen hailed their adventure as the first-ever sledge journey on the Antarctic pack ice. For him, as you will see, it would be the first of many.

The *Belgica*, having been imprisoned in the ice for almost one full year, finally broke free in February 1899, thanks to Cook and Amundsen's leadership in rousing the crew to use saws to cut a channel in the ice. The ship then sailed to the nearest port—Punta Arenas, Chile—and later back to Belgium. The expedition had taught Amundsen valuable lessons in planning, survival, leadership, and decision making in polar regions.

The question now was: how could he put all this experience to use?

Chapter 16

Planning To Succeed Where Others Had Failed

Amundsen was constantly thinking about ways he could make the Northwest Passage journey successful. He reflected on his experiences onboard the *Belgica* Expedition. One of the expedition's goals had been to chart the exact location of the South *Magnetic* Pole.

When we mention the North or the South Pole, we are talking about the geographical axis around which our world rotates—easiest envisioned as the spindle penetrating a desktop globe at the top and bottom. The North and South *Magnetic* Poles are something quite different.

The planet Earth has its own unseen, internal magnetic field. Think of this as a giant bar-magnet buried deep, capable of creating the North and South *Magnetic* poles. These are the places a compass—and the needle in every ship's binnacle or steering compass in Amundsen's day—will unfailingly point to.

In those days, the ship's compass and the celestial navigation of the sextant were the only tools that explorers and seamen had to find their way across the trackless seas. The exact location of the magnetic poles was of crucial importance.

But, as we understand much better today, these magnetic poles are not fixed places in the earth. They continually move around, making their value as a navigation tool suspect. That is why the Antarctic expeditions in the early years of the twentieth century were so important. If the exact—and here we mean exact—location of these migrating poles were not placed periodically on the map, then all ships depending on them for navigation may well come to grief as a result. Not knowing exactly where they were, sea captains could inadvertently crash their ships into unexpected rocks, reefs, or shoals, or become lost and miss ports altogether.

Determining the location of the South Magnetic Pole was one of the goals of the *Belgica* expedition, but it turned out to be too far inland for them to measure. Although the ship never came close to finding it, the search inspired Amundsen to make it one of his life's goals to locate the North Magnetic Pole. To do so, he would need to unravel the final secrets of the Northwest Passage.

Amundsen carefully studied Nansen's attempt to reach the geographical North Pole on his 1893–1896 *Fram* Expedition. Going against all conventional methods used at the time, Nansen had the *Fram* specially built to be intentionally frozen into the Arctic Sea ice. Once secure this ship, uncrushable in design, was expected to drift along with the pack ice across the North Pole. At the time, it was not clear to explorers, geographers, and map makers whether the entire north polar region consisted of constantly moving sea-ice or had land with ice and snow attached (like in Antarctica).

The *Fram* never did reach the North Pole; the drift carried it elsewhere. Its real success lay in proving that a small, well-planned, and well-manned expedition could successfully—even happily—survive years in the Arctic without any of the problems that had bedeviled the *Belgica*.

On that same expedition, once Nansen realized that the *Fram* would not get close to the North Pole, he and Fredrik Hjalmar Johansen—an explorer who will feature in chapter 19—set out to try to achieve it by dog sledge. They didn't reach it, and in an incredible story of survival, they overwintered in a primitive stone hut they built, surviving on polar bear and seal meat. When the weather improved, they traveled along the coast in their leaky kayaks thinking they could make it back to Spitzbergen in Northern Norway. But because the region was unmapped, they didn't realize that ahead of them lay an open water journey of over 100 miles (160 km). They were rescued from certain death after an unbelievably lucky encounter with the British explorer, Frederick Jackson.

Planning

Armed with knowledge of how Nansen's *Fram* expedition team survived on the ship for multiple years, and with his own Antarctic experience, Amundsen began planning his own voyage of discovery to find the Northwest Passage. But first he had to finish his obligatory military service and then go back to sea to complete his master's certificate. In the months under sail when he was off-watch, Amundsen studied polar literature, learning from the narratives of Dr. John Rae who, fifty years earlier, had pioneered the concept of a small party living off the land while exploring the vast and desolate north Canadian tundra.

Amundsen considered the survival techniques of the indigenous people living in cold regions. These included their use of sennegrass as an insulating material in footgear and the making of the highly nutritious pemmican—traditionally made from powdered, dried meat and fat. He also sought the advice of Otto Sverdrup, now veteran of two *Fram* expeditions and the foremost European expert in dog-driving.

Amundsen's methodical approach to problem solving was a trait he shared with Brunel and Roosevelt—all three men systematically planned out the steps that would lead them to achieve their goals. Amundsen determined which steps he must build upon and in what sequence, readying himself for an achievement which he alone had chosen, but for which the world would bestow upon him significant recognition and honor.

Not given, but earned

Most important among those preparations for Amundsen was to acquire impeccable credentials in magnetic observation, for only these would ensure the support of the scientific community—and the financial backing needed to carry out his program. The key to all this was identifying the true location of the North Magnetic Pole. It had first been discovered in 1831 by James Clark Ross during a sledging expedition undertaken during his uncle, John Ross's, unsuccessful expedition to find the Northwest Passage. With many sailors getting seemingly different compass readings over time, a theory had emerged that the magnetic poles were not in fixed locations on the planet. One goal of Amundsen's Northwest Passage voyage was to rediscover the location of the North Magnetic Pole, to determine if it had indeed changed.

Armed with only a letter of introduction, he traveled to Hamburg to knock on the door of the renowned physicist Georg von Neumayer, hoping for the best. The old professor, the world's leading expert in geo-magnetic research, could have turned Amundsen away. Von Neumayer, however, was so impressed with the young man's plan and his tenacity, he took on this eager and serious new student, exclaiming, "Young man, if you do that, you will be the benefactor of mankind for ages to come. *That* is the great adventure."[16]

It was quite the self-imposed program, worthy of any institution of higher education. There was much more that Amundsen would need to do in addition to studying geo-magnetic theory and measurement. The sequence of steps included building a lasting friendship with acclaimed explorer Fridtjof Nansen and learning dog-sledging skills from Otto Sverdrup. Nansen helped to open political doors, and appealed to King Oscar II for funds to support Amundsen's expedition.

Amundsen's work also included buying a ship, with his own and borrowed money. He chose the *Gjoa*, a single-masted 47 ton, former herring sloop. At 70 feet (21 m) in length, the *Gjoa* was just large enough to carry the expedition he had in mind. Experts at the time told him that the vessel was far too small for an attempt on the icy, dangerous and potentially lethal Northwest Passage.

Undeterred, Amundsen assembled a scratch crew from the sealers who were based in Tromsø, a Norwegian town north of the Arctic Circle. Together, they took his "new" ship on a five-month shakedown cruise into the ice pack off the Norwegian archipelago of Svalbard in the far north. Here he practiced the best methods of navigating the treacherous ice fields, and realized the value of having on board an experienced Arctic cook who could serve up fried guillemot for breakfast and seal ragout for supper.

Amundsen sought out six of the best, most resourceful crewmen to accompany him on his search for the North Magnetic Pole and the fabled Northwest Passage. And once he had convinced them to come along, he had to ensure their wages would be paid for the anticipated four-year-long expedition—whatever the outcome.

His crew included a lieutenant in the Danish Navy who would serve as his second-in-command, navigator, geologist and astronomer. The first and second mates had significant experience in navigating ships in icy waters. The expedition cook had years of polar experience, having worked on Nansen's *Fram*. Knowing there would have to be more than one magnetic expert on board to fully certify whatever findings they may bring home, Amundsen sent Gustav Juel Wiik, his choice for second engineer to Germany to study magnetism with Neumayer, as he himself had done. He also employed Peter Ristvedt as a meteorologist and engineer.

The scientific work would justify the expedition in the eyes of governments and academics; the final discovery of the Northwest Passage would ensure Amundsen's place in exploration history. Amundsen's attempt would be made with a crew that was ninety-five percent smaller than Sir John Franklin used on his fatal expedition, which had far more staff and supplies and required two ships to be sailed in tandem.

A historic journey begins

Amundsen had no doubt that he would succeed where Franklin had failed, but he did not have the funds for the undertaking. His creditors were hounding him, fearful their loans would go unpaid. With all other arrangements for the journey completed, on June 16, 1903, just after midnight, the *Gjoa* slipped out of Christiania Fjord and entered the North Sea. There was no jubilant send-off for these seven men, just a quiet seamanlike departure for another long and adventurous voyage.

Up to this point, Amundsen had achieved what he had set out to do—he was both captain in command of his own ship *and* leader of the expedition. One person in charge of both allowed him to adhere to his main principles: smaller was better and a single point of command would ensure consistent decision making.

The first leg, the Atlantic crossing to Davis Strait off Greenland, was so stormy, Amundsen was glad he'd taken the time to learn how his little ship would handle it. They managed to land safely, and with help from the locals in the port town of Godhavn, Amundsen and his men refilled the *Gjoa*'s holds, stacking her decks high with over a hundred cases of stores Amundsen had sent out ahead on a whaler.

On top of these were chained seventeen Greenland sledge dogs, all spoiling for a fight. If they could make it across Baffin Bay, off the west coast of Greenland, and into the Barrow Strait (which lies between the islands of northern Canada) without capsizing, the Northwest Passage could likely be navigated and conquered. Still it would be a long and hazardous journey to even get there.

Luck was with Amundsen, at least for this early part of the journey.

The weather and the seas remained clear for the crossing. The expedition stopped a few days at Beechey Island in the Canadian Arctic, where Franklin's *Terror* and *Erebus* had overwintered in 1845. Franklin and his team had left behind a pile of rusting tins as well as the graves of three sailors—the first of his men to perish in their failed quest for the Northwest Passage.

For Amundsen, this stop was a milestone in his own journey. He paused here to reflect on its significance, then consulted his dip needle (a type of compass used in measuring the physical location of the magnetic pole) to plot the best direction to steer the *Gjoa* so he could complete the scientific task he had promised to deliver: identify the true location of the North Magnetic Pole.

The dip-needle trended south but his intuition told him he needed to sail down Peel Sound on the west side of Boothia Felix—the original name of the Boothia Peninsula. This was the northernmost extension of the North American continent, and beyond the farthest point any vessel had ever penetrated and returned.

With the *Gjoa* heading into virgin waters, the task had begun in earnest.

The *Gjoa* gets into trouble

At the north end of King William Island, Amundsen followed his instincts and the compass into an unexplored strait down its east side. Would it lead into the Passage, or prove to be a dead end?

The expedition nearly came to a halt in these uncharted waters when the *Gjoa* ran hard aground, twice, on unseen shoals. The second time while the ship was hard on the rocks, a storm blew in and pounded the *Gjoa* with unabated fury for two full days, lifting the boat up and smashing it down so hard Amundsen feared it would be literally pulverized into splinters.

There was no way the ship could survive such a beating. Amundsen prepared his crew to abandon ship and take to the lifeboats, but his first mate implored him to try one more tactic. Amundsen agreed. Working with the crew, they threw 10,000 lb (4,500 kg) of dog food and everything else that could be spared, overboard to lighten the ship. Then he jammed the petrol engine hard astern. A fortuitous turn of the wind slid the *Gjoa* off the rocks.

Lesson learned. From now on Amundsen would keep the crow's nest in the upper part of the mast manned whenever navigating uncharted channels.

Another life-threatening incident occurred one night when a fire broke out near the ship's engine, next to storage drums containing 2,200 gallons (over 8,000 liters) of gasoline. Everyone aboard knew a fire could cause a catastrophic explosion, igniting the additional 4,800 gallons of fuel, along with the gunpowder and other explosives that the ship was carrying. Adding to the hazard, the wood of the ship had been previously saturated with flammable tar to preserve its decks and yards from rot. Had the fire blazed out of control, not only would the ship have been doomed, but the men too. Amundsen's team, chosen for their energy and resourcefulness, quickly took charge and doused the flames before the fire could take hold.

In early September in 1903 Amundsen and his crew sought a safe harbor in which to overwinter. Once anchored, they would need to prepare for the overland journey the following spring to locate the North Magnetic Pole. They would also immediately have to start the hunt for fresh meat to replace the tons of pemmican dog food thrown overboard to save the ship.

Amundsen nosed the *Gjoa* into a snug cove on the southeast shore of King William Land, protected from the marauding sea ice on three sides. This encampment, which they named Gjoahavn, had the added benefit of placing them in a perfect position to continue the work on magnetization.

By October 3, the vessel had become firmly frozen in and would not be freed from their encampment for at least one winter, and possibly more. Amundsen used this time to explore the surroundings and get to know—and learn from—the local Inuit people. Amundsen made sure his crew understood the importance of gaining further environmental knowledge and developing a friendship with the Inuit, during the upcoming months of bitter winter and isolation.

Learning from the best

The Netsilik Inuit there had never encountered white Europeans before.

Their ways were simple. They had no written language and their history had been handed down orally over thousands of years. They were adept at living in the privations of their environment.

From the snow, they made shelter; from local game they made every article of clothing by hand. The clothing was highly detailed and the people were so impressively efficient in the use of skins and sinew that Amundsen soon abandoned the ship's traditional wool clothing and the lower quality fur clothing he bought in Greenland, and adopted locally-made fur clothing for the remainder of the voyage.

Amundsen and his crew also learned from the Inuit people the fine art of dog-driving and the role that dog psychology played in it. Inuit dogs were not beasts of burden but equal partners in a dog–human partnership. Perhaps the most important skill to be learned was the art of patience.

In the spring of 1904, Amundsen put this newfound knowledge to work, setting off by dog sledge to find the North Magnetic Pole. But patience eluded him. Anxious to get this obligation out of the way, and with a vested interest in the scientific outcome, he and three of his crew left the ship on March 1. It was far too early in the season and the weather had not yet settled.

Bitterly cold temperatures forced them to turn back after the third night out, before Amundsen's very first northern sledge journey became deadly. Surprisingly, Amundsen would make a similar mistake on a future expedition, as we will later see. He started out again on March 16, this time with only one man, Peter Ristvedt, on a trial run to deposit some supplies along the trail that they would pick up when the real journey started later in the spring.

That third excursion departed three weeks later. Amundsen and Ristvedt started strongly but then Amundsen broke their only chronometer, an instrument critical to their magnetic studies. In a remarkable solo effort, Ristvedt returned to the *Gjoa* to get a replacement, traveling over 60 miles alone (100 km) non-stop in less than twenty-four hours, ensuring they did not lose time.

Much-improved weather conditions, coupled with the hard-won experience of the two earlier forays, resulted in twenty days of pleasant, relatively easy travel to Cape Adelaide, to the very spot where James Clark Ross had located the North Magnetic Pole seventy-three years before.

Amundsen checked his dip needle.

The pole was no longer there.

The dip needle showed that the magnetic pole had apparently shifted northward in the intervening years. The two men chased after it for three weeks, during which they established eight different magnetic stations to box it in, but never quite conclusively nailed down its precise, new, location. They did the best they could, "ringing" the elusive and invisible spot that was in those days so vital to maritime navigation.

They arrived back at Gjoahavn seven weeks later, where a careful review of the magnetic observations followed, showing that they had missed the actual spot by 31 miles (50 km). While that was a defeat for Amundsen, the scientific world would come to recognize that Amundsen's most important scientific discovery was not so much the location in geographical coordinates, but definite proof of the very fact that it could move. (Since then, the North Magnetic Pole has shifted considerably northward from the Canadian Arctic Archipelago. It is now located in the Arctic Sea, placing it much closer to the North Pole.)

Amundsen and his crew stayed in Gjoahavn for an additional twelve months. They used the time productively, exploring and charting hundreds of miles of coastline all around King William Island, Victoria Island and the straits separating them from each other and the mainland. They came to know their Netsilik neighbors even better. Amundsen found them to be the happiest, healthiest and most contented people, while living in complete isolation from the rest of the world.

His wish for them was that civilization would never reach them.

Amundsen realizes his life's ambition—so far

The ship would not be freed from the ice until August 13, 1905, almost two years after encamping at Gjoahavn. There were still many difficult, shoal-ridden miles to go before the Northwest Passage could officially be claimed.

Ahead of Amundsen's team lay the Simpson Strait, a 150 mile-stretch (240 km) of never navigated, uncharted waters leading to the next known anchorage point at Cambridge Bay, on the south shore of Victoria Land. Cambridge Bay was an important milestone for Amundsen. Once at the bay, he could rightfully claim he had "discovered" the last missing link of the full passage, because the remainder of the passage would be through already explored waters.

Amundsen later described the harrowing time he spent navigating the *Gjoa* through the Simpson Strait as the longest three weeks of his life.

The dangers to the ship and the expedition included shallow water, ice-choked narrow passages, and hidden rocks. Using only a sounding line to assess the depth of the water, they had to slow the ship to a crawl to clear the Strait safely. One sounding revealed, to their horror, that their ship's keel was barely clearing the bottom of the Simpson Strait, with only a single inch (2.5 cm) to spare. During these weeks Amundsen was so concerned with the risks they faced that he barely ate and rarely slept.

By the time the *Gjoa* dropped anchor in Cambridge Bay, Amundsen described himself as looking thirty years older due to exhaustion and malnourishment, and his skin being so weather-beaten. But there was more to be done.

While it may have seemed like success was within their grasp in terms of distance, Amundsen and his team had only reached the halfway point of the Northwest Passage. He knew that to officially claim success his *Gjoa* would need to reach the Bering Strait.

Fifty years prior to Amundsen's attempt, a search team had been sent out to look for John Franklin's failed expedition, which had begun from the Bering Strait and sailed east, making its final stop at the protected harbor they'd named Cambridge Bay. The search team never did find Franklin, but they had sailed the exact route Amundsen's *Gjoa* would now have to take, in a westward direction.

The waters immediately ahead of Amundsen had been navigated, but had been imperfectly charted, meaning that only a handful of the dangers they'd face could be mitigated. Hidden shoals, shifting ice, violent storms, and other hazards would be a certainty for Amundsen along the 1,500 mile (2,400 km) journey through to the Bering Strait before he could safely reach ice-free waters.

For Amundsen and his men though, it meant spending another winter in the Arctic ice. Their aim was to overwinter at Herschel Island, near the mouth of Canada's Mackenzie River, but they could not reach it due to ice conditions, so they were forced to overwinter at King Point, Canada. At least there they would be in the company of the American whalers.

Having conquered the Northwest Passage, achieving one of the great geographical prizes that had eluded every other expedition for hundreds of years, Amundsen couldn't wait to get the word out. At the start of winter, he embarked on a dog-sledge journey overland to Fort Yukon, where he hoped to find the nearest telegraph station. Disappointed to find none there, he continued on to Eagle City, Alaska—a combined journey of 500 miles (800 km) that he completed in two months in the depths of winter—to share his news with the world. At Eagle City, Amundsen learned that Norway had achieved its desired independence from Sweden. It was also here that he saw trees for the first time since leaving Christiana, back in June 1903.

Amundsen rejoined the *Gjoa* at King Point in March 1906 to find that the expedition's magnetic observer, Gustav Juel Wiik, was desperately ill (possibly due to a ruptured appendix). Wiik had kept the scientific work of the expedition going during Amundsen's absence, but he died shortly after Amundsen's return, sadly casting a pall on the expedition's triumph. He was buried in the expedition's magnetic observatory that Amundsen's men had built at King Point.

On August 9 the ice finally released its hold, and the *Gjoa* continued on, pausing briefly in Nome, Alaska for a jubilant reception. The cheers from the crowd brought tears to Amundsen's eyes.

He had done it.

But how to get back to Norway?

Nome was not the final stop for the *Gjoa* in 1906 due to the limited options for returning to Norway.

Amundsen and his crew could not retrace their steps through the hazardous Northwest Passage. Airplanes had only been invented three years before, and flying was so much in its infancy that no flights carried additional passengers beyond what was needed to operate the airplane. The Panama Canal was still being built by the Americans, so the *Gjoa* could not easily cross from the Pacific Ocean to the Atlantic.

Amundsen's choices came down to either:

- Sailing the diminutive *Gjoa* around the risky and storm-prone southern tip of South America and then across the widest part of the Atlantic Ocean to reach Norway, or

- Leaving his ship at a location where he and his crew could travel by train to New York, then board a regularly scheduled transatlantic ship to Europe. (Brunel's influence on this second mode of transport is revealed in a later chapter.)

Amundsen had already made his decision many years before, when he'd first planned his Northwest Passage journey.

He left Nome on board the steamship *Victoria* on September 5, which then sailed south along the magnificent Pacific coastline of Canada, and onward to America. Amundsen had traveled ahead to carry out paid speaking engagements and spread the news of his triumph. He harnessed his new fame to raise money so he could repay the creditors he had ditched over three years before, when he'd sailed the *Gjoa* out into the Christiana Fjord under the cover of darkness. Amundsen also wanted to make preparations for his crew's triumphant reception in Norway.

His men sailed the slower moving *Gjoa* southward as well, taking the same route as the *Victoria*. After its navigation around the base of the Alaskan Peninsula, the *Gjoa* would not see shore again until she landed on the beach in San Francisco. This final leg of their journey, from the Bering Strait to America, covered 3,000 miles (4,800 km). The expedition ended when the *Gjoa* came ashore on October 19, 1906, arriving six months after the devastating Great San Francisco Earthquake.

Amundsen and his crew returned to Norway as heroes.

Chapter 17

The Enduring Legacy Of Amundsen's Quest For The Northwest Passage

It had taken Amundsen, and his team in the *Gjoa*, three-and-a-half years to successfully navigate the Northwest Passage. They had persevered through all the risks and dangers that had thwarted or demolished all previous attempts. He proved conclusively that a sea transit from the Atlantic to Pacific Oceans could be made across the top of North America. It was a magnificent accomplishment.

No one had done it before, and it would be another thirty-eight years before another ship would achieve it (traveling in the opposite direction).

Amundsen's success became a point of immense national pride for Norwegians. Norway had gained its independence from Sweden in 1905, seventeen months before Amundsen completed the Northwest Passage. For a fledgling country to have claimed one of exploration's most elusive quests was an outstanding achievement and turned Amundsen into an international hero. He and a small Norwegian team had finished what the great British Navy had tried to do for generations.

Although Amundsen's Northwest Passage route did not yield immediate value for commercial shipping in the same way the Panama Canal did, it still has that potential. Today's ice-strengthened ships, equipped with the latest navigation systems and weather predicting capabilities, could allow the Northwest Passage to be used as a trading route connecting Europe and Asia for some months of the year. Those ships are double hulled, with watertight bulkheads and underwater propellers—important features that were first introduced into ship designs by none other than Isambard Kingdom Brunel, as will be explained in Chapter 22.

What you can learn from the Northwest Passage expedition to help you build better teams

- **Study everything, then draw your own conclusions.** Through his own studies, as well as learning from experienced explorers like Nansen, Amundsen became one of the world's foremost authorities on the Northwest Passage by the time he'd set up his expedition. Using this strong base of knowledge, he was able to plan the best course of action to achieve success.

- **Prepare yourself before preparing for the expedition.** In addition to learning from earlier explorers, Amundsen focused on gaining hands-on experience. He trekked across ice, snow, and mountains in Norway; at sea he gained navigational experience while attaining his captain's license; on the *Belgica* Expedition he gained crucial sledging skills and survival techniques; during the five-month practice run in the *Gjoa* he learned how to manage his ship in rough and icy seas. Preparation was his key to a successful expedition.

- **Define clear, easy-to-articulate goals for your team.** Amundsen's goals were straightforward: sail the Northwest Passage and relocate the North Magnetic Pole. Every crewmember understood the goals, and knew it would require a multi-year expedition through a cold and hostile environment. Ventures can fail because of competing, overlapping or unclear goals, and team members over-glamorizing or underestimating the risks, dangers and time scales involved in the endeavor. Amundsen worked hard to ensure this didn't happen.

- **Keep things small: small boat, small team.** John Franklin had attempted the journey with two large ships and 129 men. In contrast, Amundsen realized that success in this particular arena would depend on having a smaller crew manning a more maneuverable craft, which could navigate more easily in narrow areas and shallow waters.

- **Ensure each team member has a specific and valued role.** Amundsen personally selected a team of highly experienced people, and each one had a specific role. This gave them a purpose and ensured the team worked well together. Their complementary (but not competing) skills were necessary for the expedition's success.

Sailing the Northwest Passage today

Voyages can be booked aboard specialized, ice-strengthened ships that sail through the Northwest Passage. Ice and sea conditions permitting, they roughly follow Amundsen's route from east to west, sailing from East Greenland, across the top of Canada and arriving in Nome, Alaska. Shorter journeys covering just the eastern or western portions are also available.

The spectacular landscape contains a variety of islands, glaciers, mountains, bays, and inlets. Walruses, polar bears (diminishing in number) and other wildlife are visible along the route. You can also visit traditional Inuit villages, including Gjoahavn (now written as Gjoa Haven) in Nunavut, Canada.

The *Gjoa* arrived in San Francisco in 1906 and was hauled up onto Ocean Beach, leaving it open to the elements and vandals until 1972, when it was finally returned to Norway. A monument celebrating Amundsen and his Northwest Passage expedition stands near the western entrance of Golden Gate Park.

The ship has since been magnificently restored and is now preserved in a special *Gjoa* display at the Fram Museum in Oslo.

The dream covering at least three centuries could finally be laid to rest, but Amundsen was only just beginning his career in exploration.

Now it was time for him to attempt an entirely different, and even more ambitious undertaking.

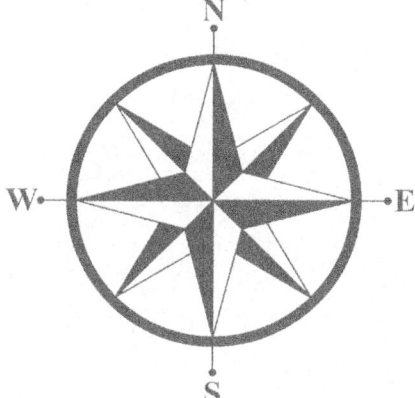

"The secret to my success has been due to self-control and willpower ... If you undertake anything, determine to accomplish your purpose and let no obstacle no matter what turn you back."

—*Roald Amundsen*

Antarctica.

Chapter 18
Synthesizing Everything You Have Learned

Reaching The Ends Of The Earth

Amundsen was still driven by polar ambition. The long years spent on the *Gjoa* had given him time to consider his next adventure. The acclaim following his Northwest Passage success had whetted his appetite for more. He wanted to seek new truths about the ice-clad extremes of the earth, and about human responses to privation, isolation and extreme cold. He would not be returning to a conventional life nor to his medical studies, only to spend the rest of his life basking in the glory for one notable achievement.

The enthusiastic response to Amundsen's whirlwind lecture tour across the United States, and the grand homecoming given to him by the government of the newly independent Norway may have been the push he needed. He and his crew disembarked from the homeward-bound mail boat at Kristiansand and boarded a naval ship there, sailing up the fjord to the new capital, Christiania, to receive a thunderous welcome upon arrival.

Later Amundsen was invited to address Britain's Royal Geographical Society—another long-sought-after dream fulfilled. Amundsen was held in high esteem and gave credit to the British sea captains, sailors and explorers who had previously attempted to find the elusive Northwest Passage. In August 1907, at the end of his triumphant year-long lecture tour through Europe, Roald Amundsen set his sights on a new geographical achievement:

The North Pole.

Vaunting Ambition?

In 1907, the North Pole had yet to be claimed, despite the attempts of the American team: Admiral Robert Peary and Matthew Henson. Somewhere up there in the swirling, shifting, floating pack ice, the pole beckoned to Amundsen, as it had to Nansen and others. Its romantic appeal—to stand on the axis of the earth's rotation while the whole planet spins *beneath* you—could not be ignored.

The lure was so strong, in fact, that Amundsen sought Nansen's support for Amundsen's application to the Norwegian government to lend him the ship Nansen had used, the *Fram*, for another attempt at the North Pole. Amundsen promised Nansen that he would complete the dream that the first drift expedition of the *Fram* had failed to manage. Nansen's own subsequent career had taken him to more staid and predictable places, something he could not abandon with the same ease as in his younger years. Amundsen persisted. Nansen's *Fram* had been built for a specific purpose: to be frozen in the Arctic drift and carried by its currents across the pole. It made no sense for it to lie idle.

Amundsen planned to sail the *Fram* from Norway, heading south across the Atlantic Ocean, around Cape Horn at the bottom of South America, and then heading northwards along the American and Canadian west coasts, to reach the Bering Strait near Alaska, where he would begin his assault on the Pole. (Roosevelt's Panama Canal could not be used as a shortcut to the Pacific side of America because it was still under construction.)

That was Amundsen's plan, until two American explorers, Dr. Frederick Cook and Robert Peary, each returned separately to civilization in the spring of 1909.

Each announced that they had reached the North Pole on separate expeditions. Cook's news appeared one week before Peary's.

Dr. Cook—Amundsen's longtime friend and mentor from the *Belgica* Antarctic Expedition—returned after two years absence in the high Arctic, saying he had reached the Pole on April 21, 1908—a full year before Peary. Cook's return journey had been much more challenging than Peary's, so it took a year longer for him to reach civilization and state his claim.

Controversy has shrouded both claims ever since.

To Amundsen it mattered little whether Peary or Cook could prove they had been there first, though he did believe Dr. Cook's claim of priority. For all practical purposes, the goal had been achieved. Its allure had faded. Amundsen's plans for the polar drift in the *Fram* suddenly had no meaning.

The ship Peary used to reach the Arctic was the SS *Roosevelt*, named after President Theodore Roosevelt. Roosevelt's own personal interest in polar exploration grew stronger when he met Fridtjof Nansen years before. During his presidency in 1908, Roosevelt went aboard the ship to wish Peary well on his journey. Upon Peary's return, Roosevelt offered to write the introduction for Peary's expedition book titled, *The North Pole*.

In that introduction, Roosevelt described the traits required to be a successful polar explorer:

"*Great physical hardihood and endurance, an iron will and unflinching courage, the power of command, the thirst for adventure, and a keen and far-sighted intelligence...*"[17]

A change of plans to meet a new reality

Amundsen had promoted his journey as a scientific expedition, with the possibility of reaching the North Pole as the icing on the cake. But actually, for him the pole was *the* goal. Without it, the expedition would amount to three years or more of being pinched in the Arctic sea ice, safe but nonetheless adrift, taking valuable oceanographic and meteorological records, but otherwise doing nothing notable or exciting. Such a voyage did not pique the interest of one of the world's preeminent polar explorers.

Amundsen changed his plan.

His new focus?

The South Pole.

It takes a certain mental agility—free from dogma, free from outdated concepts and obligations that no longer serve their original purpose—to pivot so swiftly, and so completely, toward a different goal. In Amundsen's case, a polar opposite one.

It is this trait that enables innovators to step away from tradition and with a fresh vision, forge a new reality. Amundsen shared this ability with other polar explorers of his day, including Ernest Shackleton who, time and again, showed new strength and purpose when failure and disaster seemed imminent. Amundsen also shared this trait with Brunel and Roosevelt—none of these people would let naysayers tell them what was possible, or impossible, to achieve.

Amundsen only confided his intention with his brother and his best friend. He didn't share his change of plans with Nansen, his sponsors or his crew. Nansen had helped him gain use of the *Fram* for a specific purpose: to explore the North Polar basin for which the vessel had been designed and built, and to complete the scientific work that Nansen himself had started. Amundsen had already assembled his crew for an expedition to the North Pole, and as far as they were concerned that was where they would be heading.

Much of the investment for the North Pole expedition had already been spent. Amundsen feared that if the sponsors got wind of the change they would recall their funds and Nansen would encourage the Norwegian government to rescind its offer of the ship.

So, Amundsen proceeded with raising more funds, designing a wooden hut to house him and his team, and acquiring sledge dogs. Those who doubted the wisdom of bringing a hut to be built on the Arctic drifting ice pack, or the logic of buying Greenland dogs and transporting them around the bottom of South America and north again when Amundsen could have bought sledge dogs in northern Canada, kept silent.

Adaptability in action: a new goal for a new pole

The news of the North Pole's discovery forced Amundsen to combine his two most important traits into a single, powerful response. On the one hand, his inherent flexibility allowed him to pivot—literally—180 degrees. On the other, his consummate skills in planning placed him in a good position to adapt those plans to the new goal.

This was not just any random goal, chosen simply because the opportunity presented itself. "First to the Pole" had been his objective ever since Franklin's travails in the 1800s had inspired his adolescent fantasies. Amundsen's life had been directed toward this single quest. Every step of his career—from his early days in the Norwegian highlands through to getting his mariner's licenses, from his polar expeditions in the *Belgica* first and the *Gjoa* second—had been building toward this moment. Now he was ready to claim the next big achievement.

"First to the pole." Whichever pole that may be.

The *Fram* departed Norway on August 9, 1910. Onboard was his carefully chosen crew who were expecting that in a couple of months they would have rounded Cape Horn en route to the Bering Strait at the north end of the Pacific Ocean.

When they tied up to the quay in the Portuguese island of Madeira not long into the start of their voyage, Amundsen called his crew together and gave them the startling news. (He had previously told his three officers on board.) His new plan was to divert the ship from its initial goal of the North Pole, and stop in Antarctica along the way south, to challenge the British explorer Robert Falcon Scott's attempt to be the first to the South Pole. They were welcome to go back home if they wished. But to a man, they all agreed to stay. And if all went well, they would bring another geographical prize home to Norway.

Their unanimous decision to follow Amundsen to the ends of the Earth (literally) is testament to his leadership.

National, as well as personal, pride

When Amundsen made his decision to head south, he did so with a clear reference of national pride and the idea of claiming worldwide recognition for his country. Robert Scott had already made public his intention to try for the South Pole in the Antarctic spring of 1910–1911. The British believed that it was Scott's turn after Shackleton had failed to achieve it on the *Nimrod* Expedition from 1907–1909. Shackleton's team had trekked to within 97 miles of the South Pole but had to turn back due to a lack of food. He reasoned that if his team had reached the pole, they would not have survived the return journey. Shackleton explained the decision to abandon his goal to his wife Emily, writing, "I thought you would rather have a live donkey than a dead lion."

Amundsen saw a third alternative, to be a live lion.

Amundsen was Norway's polar hero of the day. If any nation were to conquer the pole it should be his. Amundsen's determination to achieve the pole before Scott would elevate Norway into the pantheon of nations, and higher than Great Britain, the long-time claimant of multiple polar honors.

The right to try for the pole belonged to neither country. Scott and Shackleton's previous attempts had fallen short. As far as Amundsen was concerned the honor of first discovery was still up for grabs, but time was running out. Also, expeditions from Australia, France, and Germany had previously explored parts of Antarctica and one or more of those nations might send explorers to attempt the South Pole if it was not conquered in the spring-summer Antarctic season of 1911-1912.

Was it a race?

Scott's plan included much more than the nine-hundred-mile trek (1,450 km) to the South Pole, although that goal was far more important in the public eye, and for attracting donors and subscribers than the prosaic scientific studies—the geology, meteorology, glaciology and zoology of the vast, and little understood, frozen Antarctic continent. These scientific quests took up a great deal of his expedition's financial and human resources.

Scott's *Terra Nova* ship was being restocked in Australia when he received Amundsen's cryptic telegram,

"*Beg leave to inform you Fram proceeding Antarctic—Amundsen.*"

This was the first Scott had heard that there might be a race to reach the pole. Putting his trust in his chief science officer, Dr. Edward Wilson, Scott decided not to change their important scientific research program, cumbersome though it was, to focus entirely on being first to the pole.

The *Fram* was already well on the way to the Bay of Whales on Antarctica's Great Ice Barrier (an area now called the Ross Ice Shelf). It arrived there on January 11, 1911. Amundsen and his men proceeded with customary efficiency, unloading the precious cargo of dogs, sledges, food, the flat-packed hut and many other critical supplies directly onto the ice. Amundsen trusted his own analysis of the area, and ignored Shackleton's previous assessment, made on two earlier expeditions, as to the possible hazards.

To Shackleton, the ice in the vicinity had changed over time as the seaward movement of the Great Ice Barrier caused huge icebergs to calve off, but Amundsen felt that the pocket forming the Bay of Whales was sufficiently stable, especially if they set up camp a few miles inland on the ice plain.

It was a gamble but not a rash decision for Amundsen, who was sure it would hold their hut safely for the twelve to fourteen months needed for the expedition. By this point Amundsen was highly experienced in solving the problems of polar exploration. He also made sure that his preparations in men, dogs and materials were the best possible. His team trusted that the risks he took were carefully assessed, and not foolhardy.

Amundsen's attempt to be the first to the South Pole would begin shortly. But his rival, Scott, was already an experienced and accomplished Antarctic leader.

Chapter 19

False Starts, Crevasses And Letters To The King

Scott's party had the advantage of setting up his base camp at Cape Evans, a Ross Island location his team knew well from Scott's and Shackleton's previous British Antarctic expeditions.

The work of unloading Amundsen's *Fram* and Scott's *Terra Nova* ship and erecting their huts was much the same, although Amundsen's hut, which the Norwegians named Framheim, was much smaller than Scott's.

With only nine men (Scott's wintering party had more than three times that number), Amundsen's team required far less in the way of supplies than Scott's. His primary mode of transport to the pole would be dog sledges, and the dogs could be fed on locally acquired seal meat. Scott's ponies would need a regular supply of fodder.

Amundsen had set sail from Norway with ninety-seven dogs. They arrived in Antarctica with nineteen more as some had puppies along the way. He also brought with him one of the best dog sledge drivers in the world, Sverre Hassel, to manage them.

On February 4, 1911 the *Terra Nova* (without Scott and Wilson on board since they were working with others to set up their Cape Evans base) sailed into the Bay of Whales to drop off six of Scott's men who were planning to spend weeks exploring that area, including a region called King Edward VII land, which Scott had discovered and named in 1902. Since Amundsen's telegram to Scott announcing his southern intentions had not mentioned the *Fram*'s intended landing site, the crew of the *Terra Nova* were totally surprised to see another ship in the bay.

And so, by chance, the two rival teams—the British and Norwegians—met.

Scott's leader for that shore party, Victor Campbell, shared rudimentary information with Amundsen as to the location and intentions of Scott's Ross Sea shore party who were still working to establish their base at Cape Evans 400 miles (643 km) to the east. Campbell choose his words carefully, hinting that Scott's experimental motor sledges had been successfully unloaded and were performing as expected, hauling supplies over the ice with little effort. He failed to mention that one of the three motor sledges had fallen through the ice while being off-loaded from the *Terra Nova*, and was now sitting at the bottom of the Ross Sea. Campbell owed Amundsen nothing, of course, and was indignant that the Norwegian had declared a race to the pole with the slightest of advance notice given.

Campbell declined Amundsen's generous invitation to stay the winter in the area. After exchanging pleasantries, the teams made their farewells. Campbell and his five men sailed in the *Terra Nova* to a completely different, still unexplored part of the Antarctic coast.

Careful preparations for the hard work ahead

This was Amundsen at his best: organizing an expedition with a fixed and clear goal in mind, and setting up the base camp from which to achieve it. The Framheim hut had been built to his own design specifications, by his carpenter friend, in Amundsen's front yard. It was then dismantled and flat-packed for transport, ready for reconstruction on the ice.

After the unloading of the *Fram* was complete, the ship set sail on its first oceanographic survey of the Southern Ocean. Amundsen's shore party began turning their winter quarters into a snug home and efficient workshop to prepare for their upcoming assault on the pole. Every person in the shore party had been chosen for their adaptability. They were seamen and scientists, yet each could wield a hammer or a shovel as well as any man. Those who were not already well-versed in dog-sledge driving soon learned the craft moving all the supplies far enough inward to more stable ice. Although the newly formed "fast" ice at the sea edge could shear off unexpectedly, Amundsen was confident that the main ice structure would hold for at least the year he would need for the task ahead.

During the winter their hut became snowed under completely, so Amundsen's team carved a set of stairs into the ever-deepening ice. They dug a warren of tunnels and workshops below the surface to allow the men to complete the many preparations still undone. Amundsen encouraged his crew to improvise, if it led to greater efficiency. There were sledges to be assembled, tents and clothing to be stitched together, snow goggles to be tested and refined, and food and fuel to be counted out and packed for the trail. Above the ice, they hunted and butchered seals for the tons of meat they would need to feed the hundred plus dogs.

The plan was to lay depots in advance along the southern route toward the Pole, with caches of food to be stored in them for the men and the dogs, and fuel to be stored for cooking as well as warming the tent in the cold evenings on the trail. The depots had to be well marked with snow cairns and flags so the South Pole Party could see them easily once they headed out. The farthest depot on the Barrier ice that they created in the waning days of autumn lay at 82° S. latitude, 240 miles (386 km) from Framheim which was twenty-seven percent of their journey to the Pole.

Through the winter, Amundsen's men worked tirelessly during days of near-total darkness to improve the gear for the coming assault. Four hundred miles (644 km) to the west, Scott's men were busy with lectures and producing a bimonthly publication called the *South Polar Times*, as well as being entertained by magic-lantern shows. On midwinter's eve, they even put on an elaborate celebration that rivaled Christmas at home.

Scott's team may have had more entertaining or intellectual pursuits to keep them busy, but at Framheim, Amundsen's men had something Scott's men did not: a sauna.

The thought that Scott's machinery would give him a significant advantage in speed over Amundsen's dogs gave Amundsen pause for concern. If the British reached the South Pole first, then Amundsen's whole reason for absconding with the *Fram* in the first place would have been pointless. Other than some scientific and weather records that were being kept as a matter of course, the pole was his only goal. If he failed to get there first, his great legacy, hard-earned in the Northwest Passage, would be severely tarnished.

A false start

In the waning days of the Antarctic winter, Amundsen's men brought the sledges and gear out of the underground warrens of their winter workshop and up to the surface. He had planned to depart in late August, even though the detailed weather records from Scott's 1901-1904 *Discovery* and Shackleton's 1907-1909 *Nimrod* expeditions had reported August temperatures too low to survive on the trail for any extended time. Amundsen's plan was forestalled because August 1911 proved equally as cold.

The first week of September was no better, but driven by fear that Scott and his motorized sledges might already be much farther along, Amundsen could wait no longer. Against his own good judgment, he set out on September 8 with seven men and more than eighty dogs, following the old sledge tracks from the autumn's depot journeys and the line of black flags set up in advance as guides.

It proved to be one of the worst moves of Amundsen's entire career.

Their rattling pace of the start did not continue for long. With temperatures of -61 °F (-52 °C) and a breeze dead ahead, it was too much for the dogs. The extreme cold was causing frostbite on their faces and paws. In the morning the dogs refused work and had to be lifted up and put into their harness. The extremely challenging sledging conditions impacted the explorers' ability to navigate when the fluid in the compasses started to freeze. The men were suffering badly, too.

But they kept going.

On September 13, the temperature dropped further, to -69 °F (-56 °C). Amundsen brought out a bottle of Aquavit gin to cheer the spirits of his men. It was frozen solid. Unable to go farther without risking serious frostbite and death, they unloaded their sledges at 80° S, built another depot, and headed back to Framheim.

Their once-glorious start had become just another depot-laying journey—one that was never needed. They threw themselves on the now-empty sledges and raced back to the warmth and safety of Framheim. Along the way Fredrik Hjalmar Johansen had to stop his sledge to save the life of Kristian Prestrud, who was suffering badly from the cold.

It wasn't exactly a defeat, but it could hardly be described as a victory either.

After their return, Amundsen fell out with Johansen, who years before had accompanied Nansen in an attempt on the North Pole. Previously, Johansen had argued with Amundsen in front of the other men that it was too early to start. Now he was proven right, especially since they had barely survived a haphazard and disorganized return journey.

For Amundsen, the real glorious start would have to wait.

And leave him wondering where Scott was in this race.

The real start of the historic journey

Two more weeks passed, and the men waited impatiently at Framheim for the Antarctic winter to release its grip on the Barrier. They would need a steady, unbroken rise in temperature to begin and complete their historic mission. But they were not idle, constantly reworking every item of their sledging outfit.

While waiting, Amundsen decided to divide up the shore party and send a three-man team east, to have a look at the unexplored King Edward VII land. As punishment for questioning Amundsen's judgment, Johansen was unceremoniously demoted to be part of that three-man team. His fame and friendship with Nansen no longer guaranteed Johansen a place on Amundsen's South Pole expedition group.

Using similar reasoning he had used for the Northwest Passage, Amundsen decided that a smaller, leaner team of five would get to the Pole faster. By using just one tent they could get underway in half the time each morning. The depots were already laid out to within 550 miles (885 km) of the pole and were stocked for the larger original polar party.

By October 19, the day had come. The conditions had improved and looked likely to remain. Five men—Olav Bjaaland, Sverre Hassel, Helmer Hanssen, Oscar Wisting, and Roald Amundsen—driving four sledges with thirteen dogs apiece, were ready to go.

They covered 17 miles (27 km) that first day. A gale and blizzard overnight still blew hard in the morning, but their old tracks from their failed first attempt in September were still visible, so off they went. Although the long track ahead with a line of overstocked and well-marked depots was familiar to them, the way was not free of lethal hazards. Crevasses lurked beneath barely visible snow lids, ready for the unwary to fall into their bottomless depths. Near-disasters were taken lightly. Amundsen and his men were imperturbable. He had chosen them for that quality.

After four days of steady progress they had covered the first 99 miles (160 km), and decided to give the dogs a day's rest and a good feed. The cases of provisions previously left at the depots were almost entirely snowed under, but it did not take long to dig them out and chop up the frozen seal meat buried there for the dogs.

The day of rest ended with a bitter blow from the north. By morning it was too thick to even attempt a start, so they remained inside the tent all day. The amusements of eating and reading quickly lost their luster after only a few days on the trail, but the one form of entertainment that never got old was a good nap. Later that afternoon, the men rummaged through the snowed-in depot supplies and reloaded their sledges for the next leg of the trip south. With three fewer in the polar party than previously planned, three sledge loads of food and gear that had been stored during the previous depot journeys would be left behind.

They decided to take it easy en route to the next depot at 81° S, completing daily marches of 17 miles (27 km), even though their dogs could have easily covered twice the distance. They were in no hurry, knowing plenty of food was waiting for them at the next depot. Better to spare the dogs and themselves unnecessary effort.

They would need all their strength for the hard part: the unknown territory beyond, and the 10,000 foot (3,048 m) climb up to the polar plateau.

You cannot be too careful

Hundreds of miles of trackless ice and snow now separated Amundsen's five-man team from Framheim. Every mile looked the same, whichever direction they faced. Should they lose the sledge holding the navigational instruments down a crevasse, or the navigators get lost or become disabled, no one would make it home.

Survival would also depend on locating each of the depots on the return journey. If the party became disoriented by a days-long blizzard, with only the weak sun to point them in the right direction, those depots would need to be near impossible to miss. Amundsen's new plan was to mark the depots with lines of six-feet-high snow cairns (1.8 m), erected perpendicular to the trail, for a distance of a mile on each side.

South of 81°, the line of cairns was erected every 5.5 miles (9 km). Each one had a note tucked inside it, detailing its relative position in the line, and the distance and direction to the all-important depot. In total, they built 150 of these "sign posts." The extra time spent building the snow cairns was also a means of slowing their onward pace and giving the dogs a rest. The dogs would need their strength before the journey was over. Two dogs had already succumbed to the conditions.

The depot at 82° S was the last one to have been laid down in the autumn. Thanks to Amundsen's planning and unfailing teamwork, their depot laying efforts had been a success. There were plenty of supplies for the way forward and the return back to Framheim. But from this point to the South Pole they would need to load *everything* they needed—every ounce of food for the men and the dogs, every liter of fuel, the tent and sleeping bags—onto the sledges and pull them onward.

For the first time in their journey the dogs would be heavily burdened. From this point forward, the lines of snow cairns would be laid every 3 miles (5 km), as an extra measure of insurance and to allow for more rest breaks.

Into the unknown

On November 6, at 8 a.m., Amundsen and his men left the 82° S depot behind. The unknown lay before them and their work to reach the pole began in earnest. Although they were still on the level plain of the Great Ice Barrier, ahead of them was only unexplored land, never before set foot upon or seen. In every direction were windswept ice plain, riven occasionally by hidden crevasses.

But that was about to change.

Somewhere up ahead was a chain of mountains, an extension of the Victoria Range first discovered by Robert Scott in 1902, and later crossed by Ernest Shackleton on his way up the Beardmore Glacier in 1908 to reach the polar plateau. The plateau, at roughly 10,000 feet (3,048 m) above sea level, was a colder, windier and more energy-sapping environment than they had experienced on the Barrier. It could also be lethal for all the explorers in the field that spring.

Scott would be taking the route that Shackleton pioneered on his *Nimrod* Expedition. Even with a known ascent path, the Beardmore was treacherous. Motor sledges and ponies would be useless in such terrain.

Amundsen's men would be approaching the South Pole from the Bay of Whales. They would pioneer an entirely new route up whatever glacier lay before them to reach the plateau. They got their first glimpse of their challenge on November 10, 1911.

To lighten the load on their sledges, Amundsen's team laid their final Barrier depot at 85° S, planning to pick up the supplies and food on their return journey. On November 14, they reached a location where the surface of the Barrier was no longer flat but welling up in great broad waves of ice. The next day, these sweeps of ice had grown so high they blocked the view ahead. Undeterred, the men pressed on, climbing high enough to see a route forward that would take them into the mouth of an enormous glacier. They named the glacier after their sponsor, Axel Heiberg.

Amundsen and his team had made their choice. They were now committed to ascend the treacherous snow-and-ice field ahead of them.

Assessing their sledges and provisions one last time, they took only what was absolutely necessary. With the distance from here to the Pole and back roughly 700 miles (1126 km), they calculated that the round trip should be completed in sixty days.

A trip like this was no place for the tender-hearted. Everything necessary would be sacrificed to achieve the goal, including many of the dogs. Forty-two dogs were destined for the plateau, where twenty-four would be killed, butchered and fed to their canine mates. Other dogs deemed to be surplus would be killed en route to the Pole.

Amundsen's personal account of the ascent vividly describes hair-raising drops and yawning crevasses, and near-disastrous hazards quickly rising and abating. The higher up the ascent they climbed the more jagged the surface became, and the uglier the consequences of any missteps. In this location, injury and death were synonymous—they all knew that an injured man could not be carried out. This glacier was far steeper than the Beardmore, and no less rife with dangerous fields of hidden crevasses. The same gruelling work would have to be done as at Beardmore, and a similar elevation reached.

The weather remained fine, enabling the team to ascend 5,750 feet (1,750 m) in 19 miles (31 km). In the far distance, to the northwest, they saw peak after endless peak. Somewhere beyond this range, Scott might already be on the plateau, trekking toward the same goal that Amundsen desired. On November 21, with 350 miles (560 km) remaining to reach the Pole, Amundsen ordered the weakest dogs to be killed in accordance with his predetermined plan. The very act filled the men with deep sorrow. They had long since become attached to their loyal friends, but here at "the Butcher's Shop," as they called it, the grisly task had to be carried out.

Into the blizzard, come what may

Amundsen's team was unable to get going again as quickly as they'd hoped. A blinding, stinging gale roaring ferociously out of the north seemed like it might never end. After four straight days of confinement, all five men were fed up waiting, especially with the goal so near.

On the fifth day, Amundsen asked, "Shall we try it?" The proposal was no sooner made than it was unanimously agreed to. Here he saw the qualities that he most admired in his men—courage and dauntlessness, without boasting or big words. The men shared a few jokes while they packed up, and then headed out into the blizzard.

Eventually, the gale calmed and the travel became a little easier. The glacier rose and fell, down one slope for 2,500 feet (762 m)—a vertical dimension that would only have to be climbed again—with another couple of thousand vertical feet beyond that, before they would reach the South Polar plateau. Amundsen and his men stood on the glacier between the peaks of two mountain ranges, one trending from the north and the other looking southward into the distance. They named the place "Hell's Gate." (At the same time that Amundsen and his team were trying to reach the South Pole by way of Hell's Gate, the Culebra Cut, nicknamed "Hell's Gorge," was being dug to create the Panama Canal.)

Just past that point, a tortured ice-scape earned the name "The

Devil's Ballroom," and beyond that seemed to be a clear and level route.

They had reached the Polar Plateau.

The Pole itself, one of the great geo-physical achievements of the century and the finish line for Amundsen's race, was *only* about 200 miles (320 km) ahead. The ascent to the plateau, with its myriad of hidden dangers, lay behind them now.

Still, the trek ahead would not be easy. The rarefied atmosphere at 10,000 feet elevation, the extreme cold and violent blizzards could hamper their progress and cripple the dogs and the men with frostbite. At 87° S—according to dead reckoning—they could see the last of the mountain peaks to the northeast. All around them now was the snow- and ice-covered Polar Plateau, devoid of life except for these five men and their dogs.

And possibly Robert Scott and his team.

Two days later Amundsen and his men exceeded the distance of Shackleton's farthest southern point, reached in 1908. Now the record belonged to Norway, unless Scott was ahead of him. Each day's celestial navigation indicated to Amundsen that he and his crew were making steady progress to the Pole. On December 13 they were only one day away.

Amundsen worried that he would arrive to find either the British team standing on the very spot or evidence they had arrived, and were already heading back to their base at Cape Evans.

A day later, Amundsen, Bjaaland, Hanssen, Hassel, and Wisting reached the Pole. At 3pm, the dog-sledge drivers called out, "Halt!" simultaneously, their distance-measuring sledge-meters all showing they'd covered the required mileage. They had done it!

The men cheered. The weather was so fine it was like it had been planned for their arrival. Even more thrilling for Amundsen—he saw no evidence that Robert Scott had been there before them.

The South Pole

The five men made camp on the spot and raised the Norwegian flag, but their work was not done. Recognizing that their measurement equipment may not be accurate enough to precisely pinpoint the Pole, Amundsen directed his men to spend the next two days trekking out in all directions from the tent, spanning a twelve-mile radius (19 km), to make good their claim and silence any potential doubters.

By noon on December 17, 1911, they had completed the last of their observations. Amundsen was certain now that they had done everything possible to prove their claim. He left behind a tent to mark the South Pole, as well as two letters: one for Scott, the other for the King of Norway.

All Amundsen and his team had to do now was turn around and make the long trek back to Framheim, where the ship should be waiting. Before leaving, they shared a solemn moment. They took off their hats and bade farewell to both the location they had dubbed Polheim and the Norwegian flag flying above the tent.

Sixteen dogs remained, and they had enough food for eighteen days. Many risks still faced them on the return leg, including lengthy blizzards, frostbite, snow blindness, scurvy, injury, falling into a crevasse and death.

But thanks to Amundsen's expert planning, their journey back was uneventful. Even going back down the treacherous Heiberg Glacier was a familiar enough descent not to trouble them. Except for the ice-encrusted undulations, the journey was all downhill. They arrived at the old 85° depot to find that their calculations for food and supplies needed for the round trip to the Pole had been almost exactly right. The one thing they had miscalculated was their timing.

They arrived back at the depot eight days early!

This was entirely Amundsen's fault. His acute sense of responsibility for the success of the mission and the safe return of all men meant he had left nothing to chance. The factor of safety[18] in food, fuel and time required was probably double what was needed. Even though there were surplus supplies in the depots, the effort to place them out there—their insurance in case plans went awry—had not been in vain.

It is likely those unused supplies are still out there—buried in the snowfields of Antarctica and last visited by Amundsen and his team in January 1912.

On January 25, with eleven dogs pulling two sledges, the men—still hale and hearty—arrived back at Framheim after ninety-nine days and 1,860 miles (3,000 km) on the trail. Over steaming mugs of coffee, they all agreed it was good to be home again.

The ship arrived to pick them up one day later. By January 30, 1912 everything to be shipped home was on board the *Fram*. This included thirty-eight dogs—the eleven who had been on the whole expedition, and the ones who had remained behind at Framheim.

Amundsen's gamble to erect Framheim on the ice had paid off. He left the hut, and the line of unused and partially used, depots behind, and sailed immediately to Australia to announce his victory to the world. Telegrams arrived from dignitaries around the world, including King George V of England, and US president Theodore Roosevelt who sent Amundsen a telegram expressing his "Heartiest congratulations."[19]

The *Fram* remained in the southern seas to be used in other possible voyages, including to the still-under-construction Panama Canal. (The story of the *Fram* and the Panama Canal appears in a later chapter.) Amundsen and his team returned to Norway to a heroes' welcome.

Amundsen's quest for the South Pole came about because of Dr. Frederick Cook's and Robert Peary's separate claims they had reached the North Pole. But controversy over who had arrived there first remained.

Who *had* reached it first? Did either of them reach it at all? Amundsen wanted to make sure there was no such doubt with his claim for the South Pole.

To prove it, he had left two letters for Captain Scott to find. The letter to the King of Norway that Amundsen had asked Scott to deliver was controversial. For Amundsen, it would have been both insurance and proof to say that he had indeed been first. After all, Amundsen's safe return from the South Pole was not guaranteed.

Captain Scott and his team of Dr. Wilson, Birdie Bowers, Captain Oates and Edgar Evans reached the South Pole five weeks after Amundsen. Maintaining honor among explorers, Scott kept both letters, with the intention of delivering one to the King of Norway, but Scott and his men perished on their return journey. Amundsen's letter to the King was discovered along with the bodies of Scott, Wilson and Bowers, 11 miles (18 km) from one of their depots.

But that was not the end of the story for Amundsen's letter.

Lieutenant Edward Evans (no relation to Edgar Evans mentioned above) was a senior member of Scott's expedition and the sea captain of Scott's ship, the *Terra Nova*. Given his rank, he had the honor of delivering the letter to the King of Norway. It was on that Scandinavian journey that Lt. Evans met one of the king's Norwegian assistants, fell in love and later married her. Had it not been for Amundsen's letter, and Scott honoring the unwritten explorer code, Lt. Evans would never have met his bride.

Amundsen and Scott

Amundsen's great achievement—first to the South Pole—coming only six years after his magnificent discovery of the Northwest Passage, was overshadowed by the attention on Scott. At the memorial service for Scott, the King of England kneeled down in Scott's honor. This may be the first and only time a British monarch has ever kneeled at a commoner's funeral.

The death of Scott and his men caused a large outpouring of grief in Britain. To some, the tragedy was that the fallen British hero would have reached the Pole first had a Norwegian explorer not broken the British sense of a mythical explorer code, which granted Scott the right to conquer it, uncontested.

When the time came for Amundsen to be honored at a Royal Geographical Society dinner in London, he was decried in a speech given by his hosts for turning the great explorer Scott into nothing more than a letter-carrying messenger. To add further insult, they raised a toast, not to Amundsen, but to Amundsen's dogs.

Amundsen's victory would receive one final blow.

Johansen, the esteemed Norwegian explorer who Amundsen had demoted from the polar party after he'd disagreed with him, sadly took his own life shortly after returning from Antarctica. This tragic outcome was not specifically due to what happened in Antarctica, but some blamed Amundsen which further tarnished his image.

Despite all of this, we must marvel at what Roald Amundsen achieved. He was the first person to stand on the exact spot in the Southern Hemisphere upon which the Earth rotates. He proved that with expert planning, perseverance, and the right mental attitude every location on Earth could be accessible.

And that was not the end of the story for Amundsen.

After achieving the Northwest Passage and the South Pole, Amundsen searched for a new adventure. Since it was apparent to him and many others in the scientific circles of the day that neither Cook nor Peary had reached the North Pole, did that mean that it was still attainable? Amundsen's *Fram* expedition still had the North Polar drift in its schedule, but interest in the project—and the funding to complete it—was waning fast.

Amundsen was not done exploring the polar regions. Always the adaptable planner, he sought out new techniques and new technologies for his next adventure, and those came with even greater risk than his previous ventures.

Chapter 20

The Legacy Of Achieving The South Pole

To put Amundsen's 1911 achievement in perspective, the next person to see the South Pole and to get back safely was the American aviator Richard Byrd, who flew over it in 1929. (Byrd will appear again later in this book.)

The first expedition team to actually *stand* on the South Pole after Amundsen and that survived to tell the tale was one led by Vivian Fuchs and Edmund Hillary. (This was a few years after Hillary was the first to summit Mt. Everest.) Fuchs and Hillary arrived in 1958, a full forty-seven years after Amundsen. And they achieved their journey by using large Sno-Cat tracked vehicles and receiving air-dropped supplies.

Today, the South Pole is the location of the Amundsen–Scott South Pole Station, which houses the United States National Science Foundation's polar research organization.

What we can learn from Amundsen to help us attain our goals

- **Combine everything you have learned.** Amundsen learned from his polar experiences on the *Belgica* and the *Gjoa* that small, fast teams are the key to success. He also learned from the Inuit, as well as other explorers, about how to live and thrive in cold conditions.

Amundsen brought all that knowledge to his South Pole expedition.

- **Take calculated risks.** Conventional wisdom dictated that expeditions should set their hut on land because the ice surrounding Antarctica was too prone to calving or splitting. However, Amundsen had done a careful assessment of the Bay of Whales area and had drawn his own conclusion: the geography of this region meant the ice was stable and the risk was worth taking because it shortened their journey to the South Pole. Amundsen cites this decision to be part of the key to his success.

- **Leaders need to be adaptable.** The near-fatal early spring start gave Amundsen a chance to reassess his approach to achieving the South Pole. Rather than starting again with the same team a few weeks later, he took advantage of the delay to rethink his plan. Amundsen pared his eight man polar team down to five men. This ensured there would be more than enough food and supplies in the depots for the journey, since the depots had been stocked for the original larger team.

- **Plan, innovate and test.** Amundsen was constantly refining equipment, clothing, food rations, depot flags and other essentials. Like Brunel, he developed a habit of reassessing all elements of a venture and questioning all assumptions, with the aim of avoiding errors and gaining greater success.

- **When necessary, make decisions quickly.** One of Amundsen's skills on the ice was taking quick, decisive action, knowing that if a poor decision was made, it could be improved upon or reversed.

Can you visit the South Pole today?

Scientists reach the Amundsen–Scott South Pole Station by use of specialist flights originating from South America. Intrepid modern-day adventurers have reached the pole by skiing, sledging, and other means. But none can reach it by dog sledge the way Amundsen did—dogs were banned from Antarctica in 1994 under the Antarctic Treaty prohibiting non-native species.

Other parts of Antarctica can be visited on specialist ice-strengthened cruise ships traveling from South America to the Antarctic Peninsula, or from Australia and New Zealand to the Ross Sea and Bay of Whales regions. Framheim no longer exists.

It is a thrilling experience to walk on the deck of the *Fram*. The ship can be found in its own museum in Oslo, where you can also see many artifacts from that era, as well as displays about Amundsen. The Fram Museum regularly wins awards for the best museum in Norway. The Holmenkollen Ski Museum in Oslo houses an impressive collection of skis and other polar equipment from both Nansen's and Amundsen's expeditions.

Amundsen's letter to the King of Norway is stored in the National Archives of Norway.

Brunel, Roosevelt and Amundsen: Monumental achievers

All three people—Brunel, Roosevelt, and Amundsen—possessed a staggering amount of energy, far more than the ordinary person it would seem. How else can we explain their restlessness, always on the go from one place to the other, and switching from one idea to the next?

In the next chapters we reveal more insights that come from looking at their work and personalities, and describe what Brunel, Roosevelt and Amundsen did next in their life-long quest to set audacious goals and their desire for truly remarkable results.

Part Four

Enduring Lessons

"Never throughout history has a man who lived a life of ease left a name worth remembering."

—*Theodore Roosevelt*

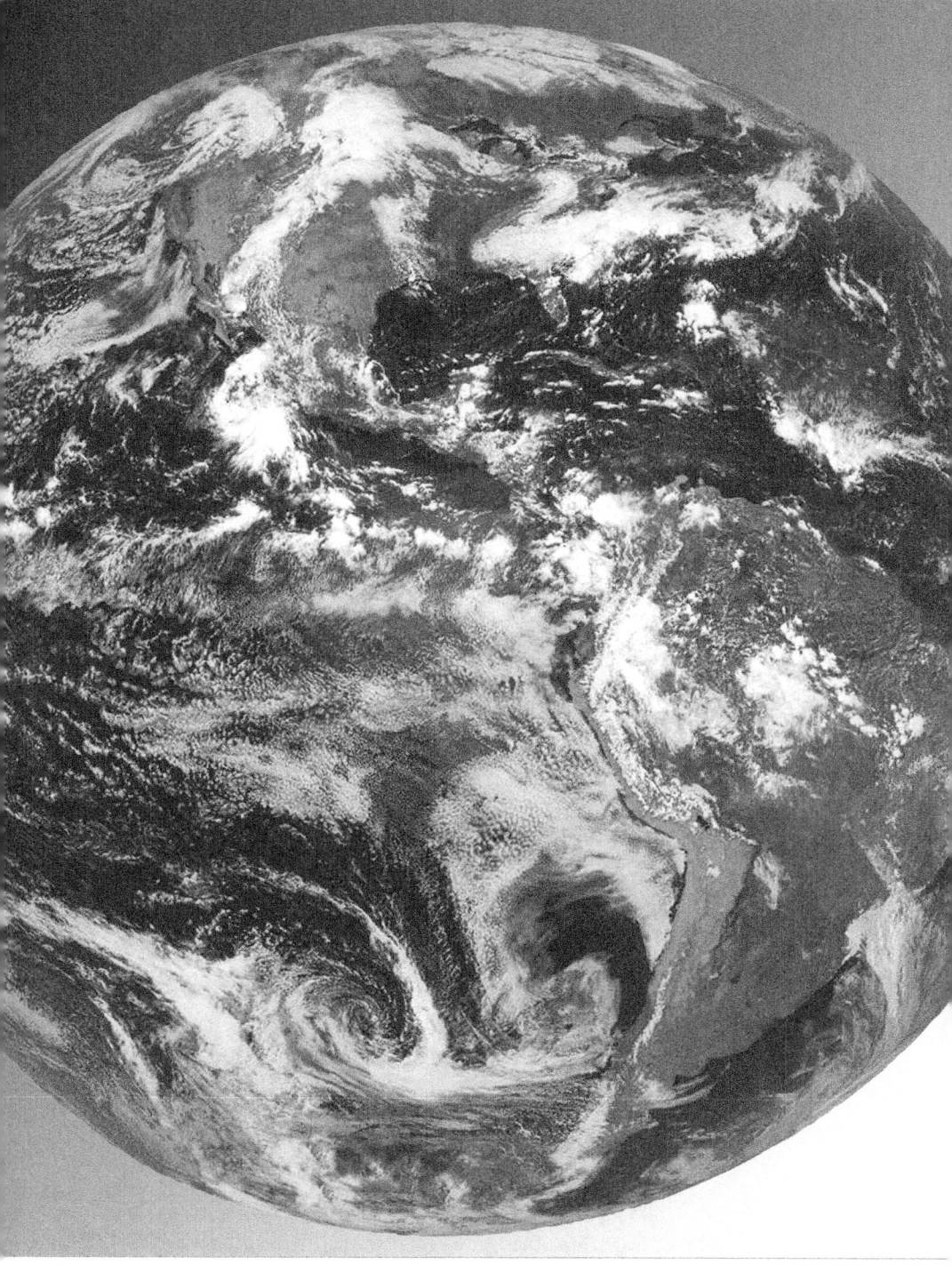

Chapter 21

Ten Lessons From An Explorer, An Engineer, And A Statesman

Here are ten further lessons we derived from examining the projects and these visionaries together. This list is certainly not exhaustive. As you read through them, it might be helpful to keep these questions in mind:

"What would I have done if I'd been in their shoes?"

"What other lessons can I learn from Brunel, Roosevelt and Amundsen that I might bring into my own life?"

1. **Think big.** Have bold goals. To succeed in a big way requires a grand vision and ambitious goals. One of the traits Brunel, Roosevelt and Amundsen shared was that expansive thinking brought them bigger rewards.

2. **Patience is vital.** Great endeavors take time. The accomplishments in this book spanned years and decades:
    - Thames Tunnel: eighteen years
    - London to Bristol Railway: six years
    - Panama Canal: eleven years
    - Northwest Passage: three-and-a-half years

    Achieving audacious goals can be a multi-year process. To

gain success, Brunel, Roosevelt and Amundsen kept their focus on both the end-goal, and even more importantly, on the benefits that achieving the goal might deliver. For example, a train line that could deliver faster and better transportation across Britain, and US national forests and parks enabling families to enjoy protected spaces for generations to come.

Staying focused over a period of time requires resilience and endurance, and an ability to think laterally as obstacles are encountered. How did they achieve their goals? By enjoying the journey as much as the destination.

3. **Master the details.** Brunel, Roosevelt and Amundsen led from the front—working as hard, or harder, than everyone else around them. Brunel pushed his projects forward by spending long hours in the field. This gave him an on-site, hands-on understanding of the task.

   While Roosevelt's presidential duties meant that he could not be in Panama on a regular basis (in those days, US presidents did not travel outside the USA—Roosevelt was the first to break that tradition by going to Panama to see the construction), he made crucial decisions about the Canal after careful consideration of the choices presented to him. Amundsen was also intimately involved in every decision and detail of his expeditions.

4. **Physical, political and financial risks are all part of success.** These trailblazers were not daunted by the physical dangers or personal hardships their endeavors attracted. They also did not fear the risks arising from high profile setbacks and failures associated with their visions—failures that risked the loss of future funding, or royal or government support.

   The men faced dangers on a daily basis: Brunel's work in the tunnel, Roosevelt's service as a Rough Rider, and Amundsen's time on every expedition he led. Politics overshadowed all of their projects and failure or success was front page news. Amundsen (and later in life, Brunel) also risked their own financial security to achieve their visions. To them, risk was just part of the adventure.

5. **Success requires great teams and partnerships.** Brunel, Roosevelt and Amundsen all understood the value of building strong teams around them. Brunel worked closely with his engineering assistants on the Thames Tunnel, and later with Daniel Gooch on the locomotive design. Roosevelt aligned with great people like John Muir and George Bird Grinnell to protect the wilderness and forests of the United States, and brought in trusted men like John Stevens, Dr. Gorgas and George Goethals on the Panama Canal project. Amundsen sought out world-renowned experts in multiple fields on his *Gjoa* and *Fram* journeys, and gained Dr. Frederick Cook and Fridtjof Nansen as mentors.

6. **Failure is part of the process.** This may be easy to say but it is not so easy to experience. Accepting failure is hard. Brunel bounced back from the tunnel flood disaster and from the poorly performing tracks and locomotives he designed. Roosevelt had to "eat humble pie" when John Stevens told him that his make-the-dirt-fly initiative was a failure, a sea-level canal was not possible, and the change to a lock-based canal meant that at least half of the dig by the French, for which the United States had paid so much, could not be used. Amundsen's premature start to the South Pole and the haphazard return from it almost cost some of his men their lives.

7. **Continuously learn and adapt.** Brunel, Roosevelt and Amundsen emulated chess players when planning their projects—often thinking five, ten or twenty moves ahead, assessing pitfalls and mitigating risk. They adjusted as they learned more about tunnels, trains, land preservation, canal

construction, and polar climates and their terrains. Every endeavor they embarked on led to new insights and better ways of working.

8. **Find your passion.** Love what you do. A common trait these three leaders shared was a deep passion and love for the work. The end goal stirred their soul and drove each of them to work longer hours than the timetable dictated. Shortcuts were never taken. Long hours and difficult decisions were part of the thrill. These individuals did not view weeks the way we do now, as five days on, interrupted by two days of rest and relaxation. Each day brought them closer to their achievements.

9. **Build new successes by reassembling and combining.** These three men were innovators whose greatest accomplishments lay in reassembling ideas that were already in existence. Brunel did not invent the steam engine, or the idea that the fastest railway would be the most level, or that iron could be more efficient than wood in the construction of ship hulls. Roosevelt did not invent the idea for national parks, or the transit of goods through canals and locks. Amundsen did not invent the dip-needle, dog sledge travel, or the ice-resistant ship for polar exploration.
All three of them instead pulled together components from sources and inventions that already existed to create their great accomplishments. Their genius lay in recognizing what was already at hand, and reassembling and combining these pieces in new ways.

10. **Have the next big, audacious goal in your sight.** Brunel, Roosevelt and Amundsen worked hard their entire lives, never resting on their laurels for long before seeking the next goal or big adventure.

And that's the topic of our next chapter.

Chapter 22

They Never Stopped Achieving

The most important trait Brunel, Roosevelt and Amundsen shared was quite simply: they never stopped achieving.

All three had boundless energy and a restless intellect that pushed them to seek out new ideas, new approaches and new solutions to age-old problems. For them it was not a matter of "what have I done," but, "what can I do next?"

"Where is the next big challenge, and how can I solve it?"

They were not driven by money, or even power. It was for the love of the endeavor, as well as their belief that they were the best person to achieve it.

Brunel—The Shipbuilder (not just of any ship, but the largest in the world)

For Isambard Kingdom Brunel, each idea led to another, allowing him to build on successes and abandon failures along the way. Even before he'd finished the Great Western Railway connecting London to Bristol, his next dream was to build a fast, reliable ship that could sail efficiently from the port of Bristol to New York. This would fulfill his dream of building an almost seamless train-and-ship link connecting London to New York City.

In the early 1830s, transatlantic ships used a combination of traditional sails and coal-powered steam engines; the latter was needed to turn paddle wheels mounted to the sides of the ship when sail and wind power were not enough. Journeys across the ocean were long, rough and unpredictable. As a result, packet ship lines were unable to keep to dependable schedules of arrivals and departures.

All of the shipbuilders of the era believed that the solution was *not* building larger vessels with more powerful engines. They thought that the engines required would consume coal at a rate proportional to the ship's bulk. Stated another way: they were certain that because a ship was bigger, all the extra space on the ship, theoretically available to accommodate more paying passengers and cargo, would in fact be needed to store coal for the larger steam engines required to power such a vessel.

In one of many great moments that proved Brunel's genius, he recognized the fundamentally unsound mathematics behind this fallacy. To prove his theory, he offered his services as consulting engineer to the newly created Great Western Steamship Company for free.

Working alongside others, Brunel designed a steamship made out of oak that had both sails and side-mounted paddle wheels. The SS *Great Western*—the sea-faring extension to the Great Western Railway—was (in typical Brunel fashion) the largest ship ever built at the time.

The ship was launched in 1838 to immediate acclaim and success, just the way he intended. The maiden voyage made the fastest ever passage to New York and was so efficient that when it arrived in the New York harbor it still had 200 tons of coal left on board, proving to all his skeptics the validity of Brunel's calculations.

In contrast, a rival company wanted their steamship to be the first of its type to complete the journey. Their ship, the *Sirius*, set out to arrive in New York before the *Great Western*. With a head start, the *Sirius* did reach New York first, but had not been anywhere near as efficient on coal usage. Its crew had to burn wooden pieces from the ship, such as furniture and internal fittings, to complete the journey!

One of Brunel's most noteworthy overachievements related to the *Great Western* was not the ship's enormous size or its destination, or that it was a continuation of a rail journey from London. It was that from 1835 until 1838, while Brunel was working on the ship's design and construction, he was simultaneously working on the London-to-Bristol railway line, which was still being built. As shown in the timeline at the end of the book, the year 1838 for example was the same year his Maidenhead Bridge was put into service; the Box Tunnel was still under construction; initial tests of locomotives were being run on the London-to-Maidenhead section of the train line, revealing major flaws that needed immediate correcting.

The *Great Western*, with its combination of size, powerful steam engines, paddlewheels and sails, was the first ship capable of meeting approximately scheduled crossing times. Before Brunel's ship that journey would have taken a month. Now the sailings took less than half that time. In its eight years of service, the *Great Western* completed sixty-seven journeys; the fastest was achieved in just over twelve days.

Here we have the pioneer who helped build remarkable tunnels and bridges, and changed railways and rail travel forever, and now he's just turned his hand to transforming passenger ships. But where ships were concerned, he was only just getting started.

The first luxury ocean liner: Brunel's SS *Great Britain*

Recognizing that paddle-wheel technology was inherently inefficient for overseas transport, Brunel next designed the first screw-propeller-driven ocean-going iron ship, the *Great Britain*. Brunel was wading deeper into the uncharted waters of creative maritime design.

Iron ships and other propeller-driven vessels existed at the time, but Brunel's new ship design was the first to combine these two new marine technologies. His bold move influenced the future design of all transoceanic ships built since the launch of the *Great Britain*.

Six years in the making, the ship was far larger than any that had previously been attempted. It was twice as big as the *Great Western* and had the most powerful engines ever installed on a seafaring vessel. Under Brunel's leadership, the *Great Britain* became the world's first great luxury ocean liner and set the standard for passenger service. It even served its own blend of champagne on board.

Brunel had perfected the art of building an iron ship. As a shipbuilding material, iron had many benefits over wood: it was lighter, stronger, and cheaper. It enabled the ship to have a thinner hull which required less cross-section strengthening. And, the cross-section strengthening it did need could be lighter in weight.

All of this meant an iron ship could hold more cargo and passengers than a comparably-sized wooden ship, making each journey more profitable. By cleverly using iron for the cross-sections needed to strengthen the ship, Brunel was able to partition the ship into watertight bulkhead sections—a valuable safety feature that can prevent a ship from sinking if the hull is pierced in one location, because one bulkhead can flood, but all the others could stay intact and free of water.

This design element has been included in every ship built since the *Great Britain*. If that had been Brunel's only achievement in his entire life, it would still have had a significant impact on the world. But there was much more to the *Great Britain*.

The challenge in all previous designs, including Brunel's first ship, the *Great Western*, was how to provide enough energy to turn the large paddle wheels on either side of the ship. (Side paddle wheels were not only a disadvantage on passenger ships, they were also an extreme point of weakness on warships. Their position and prominence made them easier for an enemy to attack.) So, Brunel perfected the underwater propeller.

He designed a six-blade screw propeller that was so efficient, modern computers could only make it five percent better than the design he created on paper, over 180 years ago. For the propeller's size and weight, which was far less than side paddlewheels, it delivered considerably more thrust.

An even greater challenge: Can one ship do it all?

After the success of the *Great Britain*, there remained one additional challenge for Brunel to solve. At the time, no steam-powered ship could hope to travel longer distances (from Europe to Asia or Australia) without having to stop to refuel. As a result, coaling stations had to be established and stocked along shipping routes in various locations around the world, brought there as bulk cargo in sailing ships. The entire scheme was a model of inefficiency: delivering coal in slow vessels to be picked up by faster or larger vessels.

If only there was a ship so large it could carry all its own fuel, as well as paying passengers and cargo, to and from any port in the world, no matter how distant. It required a solution that only the most expansive of design thinkers could envision. Enter Brunel with his proposal to build a ship to do just that—yet another first-ever, largest-ever project.

Such a ship would have to be enormous by the standards of the day. As his idea for the *Great Eastern* unfolded in his sketchbooks in the 1850s, it became clear that this ship would need to be six times the volume of the largest vessel then afloat, which not surprisingly happened to be Brunel's iron, propeller-driven *Great Britain*.[20]

His great iron ship took shape on the shore of the River Thames at a construction site that was a short walk from the Thames Tunnel, completed fifteen years before. The ship was so huge—almost twice the length and, at 12,000 tons, five times the weight of any previous ship—that ordinary machinery could not launch it. This was the largest and heaviest object ever needing to be moved up to that time, and it simply would not budge. Its launch was delayed nearly four months while new technologies in metallurgy were perfected to forge stronger chains that were up to the task.

The *Great Eastern* was not just a larger version of the *Great Britain*. It featured a new development by Brunel—one that can be found on many ships today: a double hull. If the outer hull is ever pierced, the second hull will prevent the ship from sinking. To ensure utmost speed, it needed a combination of technologies: enormous side paddlewheels, an underwater screw-propeller, and seven masts.

Reminiscent of how the length of the Great Western Railway line revealed a new problem: the need for a national definition of time, the length of the *Great Eastern* also revealed a new problem: how could the captain, engineers and ship workers communicate to each other along the length of such a huge vessel while it was en route? The traditional, cone-shaped, speaking trumpet would not amplify one's voice enough.

This communication issue was solved by using a series of colored lights connected to specific commands, and a self-contained electric telegraph system for longer messages. (While wrestling with these problems, Brunel was also designing magnificent bridges for the Great Western Railway network, like the double-span suspension bridge at Saltash, near Plymouth, which also required Brunel to think up a novel way to lift the bridge sections into place high above the river during construction.)

After a number of successful voyages, disaster struck the *Great Eastern*.

During an 1862 voyage to New York, the *Great Eastern*'s deep hull hit an area of uncharted rock that other keels had simply floated over in the past. Since the ship was so much larger than any existing dry dock could accept, new ways had to be developed to repair the iron hull of a ship while afloat. While the *Great Eastern* never achieved the success Brunel had hoped for, it was still a critically important ship that influenced future ship designs.

Years later, Daniel Gooch, who had first worked on the Great Western Railway to redesign Brunel's failed locomotives, was part of a company that bought the *Great Eastern*. Gooch helped the ship find a significant place in maritime history as the only one large enough to lay the first transatlantic telegraph cable.

Laying the transatlantic cable was one of the eleven big projects we first looked at when planning this book. This means that Isambard Kingdom Brunel was associated with *three* of our eleven initially selected projects, as described in the *Introduction*.

The three ships

The ships were the embodiment of Brunel's brilliance. Throughout history, many other shipbuilders built more ships than Brunel, and had longer careers designing sea-going vessels. However, it is possible that throughout history no other set of three ships, designed by one person, equaled the number of important innovations and magnificence showcased in the *Great Western*, *Great Britain* and *Great Eastern*. These three ships came from one great mind, brought to fruition through extensive engineering experience, strong ambition, boundless energy, coupled with a bold and fearless vision.

What Brunel accomplished is even more impressive when you consider that these were the *only* ships he ever designed. He didn't have years of apprenticeship as a ship designer to perfect his art.

Brunel anticipated the demand of future global trade. His ability to bring projects from his drawing board to completion laid the groundwork for the building of vast networks of cities, suburbs, railways and transoceanic travel and commerce by which we live today.

The enduring legacy he left behind showed others that if a tunnel, a railway, a ship, or a network of global commerce can be imagined, it can be accomplished.

What happened to the ships?

In later years, the *Great Britain* was converted to a cargo ship. Its final mission had the intention of sailing from Penarth in South Wales, around the base of South America and onward to San Francisco with a cargo of coal, a journey it had completed successfully before. The ship was damaged by a minor fire in 1886 while in the South

Atlantic. Then, on the same voyage, a storm near the Falklands nearly destroyed it.

Towed to an anchorage in the Falkland Islands, the *Great Britain* remained there for many decades as a slowly decaying hulk. The hull was rescued in 1970 and brought back to the United Kingdom where it was beautifully restored. It is now on display in the dock of Bristol, where the ship was originally built. It is the most visited tourist attraction in Bristol.

To commemorate its time in the Falklands, one of the original masts from the ship is on display in a waterfront park, in the capital city of Stanley.

The *Great Western* and *Great Eastern* ships no longer exist, but the site where the enormous *Great Eastern* was constructed, along the banks of the River Thames, still exists as a historical site. The large wooden beams that the ship sat on before entering the water are still visible.

Roosevelt—The Statesman Turned Explorer

Theodore Roosevelt was likewise gifted with a restless intellect. You might think that at the conclusion of his second term as President of the United States in 1909, having protected the vast wildernesses of the nation, having begun the process of joining two oceans with the greatest shipping link yet devised, and having brought his country into prominence as a world power—all while championing a forward-thinking domestic policy—he might have been content to rest on his laurels.

Roosevelt was far too active for that.

Immediately after leaving the White House, he embarked on a lengthy African fair chase hunting safari that segued into a European tour, where he engaged in semi-official meetings with heads of state. The African part was dubbed the Smithsonian-Roosevelt African Expedition. Operating under the guise of being officially there to collect specimens for taxidermy for the Smithsonian Institution, and for other scientist's research purposes, Roosevelt and his son killed over 500 animals, including seventeen lions, three leopards, eleven elephants and twenty rhinos. A shocking total by today's standards.

Like many of Roosevelt's hunting adventures, this one helped raise awareness for the need to protect African wildlife habitats, to ensure the longevity of species that were prized as hunting trophies.

When war with Mexico threatened in 1910, Roosevelt felt the need to serve his country once again, but his offer to serve as a Rough Rider was declined. Unhappy with the unfolding political events he began touring the country, giving speeches on the reforms being proposed by a burgeoning progressive movement, imparting the ideas that had always been close to his heart. Was it time for a third party in the United States, one closer to the people than either the Democratic or his own Republican Party?

He could resist the urge no longer.

At the beginning of the presidential election year 1912, he announced "My hat is in the ring." Through the summer of 1912, he campaigned as presidential candidate of the new Progressive Party. Roosevelt was on his way to give a campaign speech in Milwaukee on October 14, 1912 when he was shot (described at the start of Chapter 7). He survived and continued campaigning but did not win.

The expedition to the River of Doubt

Failed political attempts aside, Roosevelt had no intention of retiring from an active life.

Continuing with his lifelong interest to study the natural world up close, he organized a 1913 expedition to the Amazon River basin, which included a plan to collect specimens for the American Museum of Natural History. At fifty-five, his body—still carrying the Milwaukee bullet that doctors deemed too risky to remove—might have been past its physical prime, but his adventurous heart was not.

Once in the Amazon basin, Roosevelt declared that his original plan was too timid. With a team of explorers and scientists, which included one of his sons and the famous Brazilian explorer named Cândido Rondon, he set out on what they anticipated would be a two-month journey along the River of Doubt, a tributary and region never before explored except by the indigenous people. Traveling in dugout canoes, the team risked death from malaria, dysentery and miles of rough and treacherous rapids. They hacked portage trails through dense jungle, and sometimes dodged arrows being shot at them by the local inhabitants.

The hazards of the expedition took a toll on everyone involved. They explored and mapped over 900 miles (1450 km) of territory along the river basin, but the expedition was not a total success. One man drowned, one was murdered and another went insane. Roosevelt nearly died from jungle fever and an infection to a leg wound. When they emerged from the jungle seven months later, the world was on the brink of World War I. But for Roosevelt, there was a triumphant moment in addition to surviving the jungle ordeal. One of the projects he fought so hard for, the Panama Canal, now ten years in the building, was soon to be completed.

After returning to the United States, Roosevelt kept up his writing— publishing articles, books and his autobiography, without stopping. He even volunteered his services again when the United States became involved in World War I. His ambition was to lead troops in France, but Woodrow Wilson, the president at the time, turned down his offer.

After the war, there was even talk of his nomination as a presidential candidate for the 1920 election, but the bullet and his niggling injury from the Amazon trip impacted his health. Despite all these life challenges, Theodore Roosevelt never stopped striving for more.

Roosevelt showed that having a strong will, coupled with a steely focus, were important determiners of success. Given his family's wealth, he could have lived a life of leisure. Instead, he left the world with an inspiring variety of magnificent achievements.

Years later, the River of Doubt was renamed in his honor to become Rio Roosevelt (Roosevelt River).

Amundsen—Another Pole to Conquer

Like Roosevelt, Roald Amundsen was consumed by the thirst for adventure. Like Brunel, Amundsen shared a drive for boldness.

The Norwegian explorer didn't stop after he had achieved the goals of his life, at a time when most people would have taken a well-deserved rest. After returning from Antarctica in 1912, there were no more poles to conquer—or so he thought. The North Pole had been claimed by Cook or Peary (although it was still being debated) and the South Pole was his own. The Northwest Passage belonged to him. He was a hero to many in his native Norway, but heroism and accolades were only part of his ambition.

There was the science, too. His friend and mentor, Fridtjof Nansen's theory of Arctic polar drift had yet to be fully investigated, and there was much to be learned from a new expedition to the northern ice pack to monitor its shifting patterns. Nansen had originally built the *Fram* for such a drift and it had been lent to Amundsen for that purpose, not for a side-trip to the South Pole, no matter how successful it had been.

In anticipation of the drift expedition, and keen to explore the newest tool in the explorer's kit, Amundsen took up aviation. Amundsen had been introduced to flying while lecturing in America, when his first flight in a primitive machine convinced him that here lay the future of exploration. Flying over rough terrain would offer an unimpeded view of the world below.

Amundsen ordered two seaplanes for the upcoming *Fram* Arctic drift expedition. The journey was based on his original, pre-South Pole plan: to sail up the west coast of South America and North America and enter the Arctic from the Bering Strait.

The *Fram* was already in the southern hemisphere in 1913 and sailing toward Buenos Aires when the captain was invited to be the first to sail through the Panama Canal—with explorers Amundsen and Peary on board for the celebration. In anticipation of such a crossing, the *Fram* made it as far as Colón, Panama where, if all went according to plan, Amundsen and Peary would board, and the ship would sail through to the Pacific Ocean. It would then sail along the western coasts of the United States and Canada into the Arctic. The timing however was too optimistic for the finishing of the dig at the Culebra Cut (and the filling of the greatest artificial waterway on the planet), but it was an exhilarating thought.

With World War I looming, the Arctic drift expedition was delayed. Amundsen sold the airplanes and the ship was laid up. When he paid an inspection visit in 1913, he was shocked at what he found. The *Fram*, never intended for long exposure to warm southern waters, was in a terrible state and no longer seaworthy for a journey as ambitious as an Arctic drift voyage.

Amundsen—the shipbuilder

Amundsen needed a new ship to battle the pack ice, so he designed one using the principles of hull shape and strength that had worked so well in the *Fram*. His new ship, the *Maud*, named after the reigning queen of Norway, was launched in 1918.

The following year it headed east, traveling along the northern shore of Russia. Amundsen's aim was to reach the Bering Strait by sailing the *Maud* through the Northeast Passage, which is located off the northern coast of Siberia (a route first pioneered by a Swedish explorer) with the intention of becoming beset in the pack ice there and beginning an Arctic drift across the north polar basin.

This drift would have completed the original work of the *Fram* that was interrupted by Amundsen's stop in Antarctica for the South Pole.

Amundsen was not on board all that time; he was busy shuttling back and forth overland, engaged in other activities around the globe. On one of his journeys, he purchased two airplanes intended for the expedition's use. The planes were used for a few flights, one of which ended in a crash landing. These were some of the first polar flights ever undertaken.

In all, it took seven years for the *Maud* to reach Alaska in August 1925. She never came near to achieving the drift that had been intended for her, so had not been directly over the North Pole. The expedition did, however, achieve its scientific goals, and Amundsen and his crew member, Helmer Hanssen from the *Gjoa* who was also on the *Maud*, became the first men to sail successfully through both the Northwest Passage and the Northeast Passage.

New ways to reach an old goal

Roald Amundsen's embrace of aviation technology soon fostered a new goal: airborne exploration of the north polar basin, and the North Pole itself. A record-setting, non-polar flight in December 1921 by another pilot and crew, who flew for twenty-seven hours in the air without refueling, gave him a new idea. He wanted to fly across the entire polar basin, from Spitsbergen, Norway to Point Barrow, Alaska.

The idea was daring, but some risk was mitigated by airplane technology which was rapidly advancing in the early 1920s. Propeller-driven airplanes had become relatively efficient and reliable. The challenge was that, despite Cook and Peary's dubious claims about their treks (still being contested at that time), the vast majority of the Arctic was still *terra incognita*. If a problem did occur on an Arctic flight, absolutely no rescue would be possible, but that type of risk was common to all of Amundsen's exploits.

As with his previous expeditions, Amundsen found some scientific and geographical justification for his plan. While on a lecture tour in the United States he made the acquaintance of Lincoln Ellsworth, a wealthy individual who agreed to finance and join him on the aeronautical expedition. Amundsen proposed that two planes and two crews would take off together from Spitzbergen in the Norwegian archipelago now known as Svalbard, and land together at the North Pole to confirm observations, before proceeding onward to Alaska. The planes were named *N24* and *N25* (quite different from the exotic names that Brunel's early locomotives had, like *Firefly* and *Lord of the Isle*).

This was uncharacteristically haphazard planning on Amundsen's part. The man who had set out so many snow cairns and advance depots in Antarctica en route to the South Pole, was entrusting the success of an entire expedition on the vagaries of shifting sea ice—unlike the South Pole in Antarctica, there was no stationary continental land mass at the North Pole. The northern sea ice was floating and unpredictable in thickness and consistency.

The plan and the risks might have looked good on paper, but in practice were not good at all.

The take-off was fine, but they failed to reach their goal of landing at the North Pole, and instead landed on a different stretch of the Arctic pack ice, near 88° N. One of the planes, *N24*, was severely damaged during the landing, and with only three weeks' worth of food, it looked as though they were all doomed. The six men spent those weeks on the floating ice during May 1925 on two key tasks: leveling a runway over the shifting ice, and removing everything that was not absolutely necessary from the undamaged aircraft.

When the runway was ready and all six on board, *N25* barely lifted off, and just made it back to Spitsbergen.

Still seeking that elusive goal

Amundsen's dream of flying over the North Pole was not yet finished. An Italian dirigible—a lighter-than-air craft—was available, and it came with its Italian developer and pilot, Umberto Nobile. It was a different type of air travel. It meant trading the known problems of airplane engines and landings for the unknown problems of a lighter-than-air vessel in the extremes of the polar cold and wind. There would be less left to chance though, since the dirigible *Norge* would not have to land. It would just fly over the pole.

But they weren't the only ones interested in flying over the North Pole. Nor were they alone in choosing Spitsbergen for a take-off point during the summer of 1926. Richard Byrd, an American aviator, showed up that May in his Ford Trimotor aircraft with the intention to be the first to fly over the North Pole. Amundsen was not one to back down from a challenge, but still haunted by how he was perceived in preempting Scott to the South Pole, he graciously held off his departure so Byrd could go first. If Byrd failed to return, the *Norge* would have to rescue him.

On May 9, Byrd flew a round trip, claiming to have flown over the North Pole. He returned to the United States a hero.

Then it was Amundsen's turn.

On May 11, the *Norge* lifted her crew of sixteen, which included Oscar Wisting who had been on Amundsen's South Pole expedition, into a cloudless, blue sky and set off for the North Pole 745 miles (1,200 km) away, and Nome, Alaska on the far side of the world.

On May 12, 1926, the *Norge* crossed exactly over the North Pole. Beyond it, they saw the uncharted expanse of drifting polar ice that had long bedeviled those who'd attempted to cross it by sea and sledge. Ice began to form on the surface of the dirigible, dragging it down with its weight. The ice threatened to break off in shards and puncture the outer fabric and the inner gasbags keeping the airship aloft. In the extreme cold the ship rose and plummeted; the pilot barely kept it under control. After four harrowing days, they set the ship down 100 miles (160 km) north of Nome.

Having survived that ordeal, Amundsen traveled the following year to the United States. Interestingly a photograph exists, taken in May 1927, showing Amundsen standing in front of Theodore Roosevelt's Maltese Cross cabin in North Dakota.[21] Although Roosevelt had passed away eight years before, each would have been keenly aware of the other's endeavors.

But at the age of fifty-four, Amundsen was not done with the Arctic, and it was not done with him. The flight of the *Norge* had ended in a public relations debacle, with a dispute between Nobile the Italian pilot and Amundsen the Norwegian explorer as to which man deserved greater credit. Nobile was trying to recover some prestige for his homeland with another expedition to the North Pole in his own airship, the *Italia*. He took off in late May 1928, and didn't return as scheduled.

Amundsen, the polar aviator, went immediately to the rescue.

On June 18, Amundsen and a small crew took off from Tromsø,

Norway in a French biplane. Their destination was Spitzbergen. Once there, their aim was to fly onward seeking out the *Italia's* crash site.

Though it was a known route, Amundsen and his crew never made it to Spitzbergen. They perished in the first ever attempted polar air rescue. Later, Nobile and some of his crew were rescued.

In 1996, Byrd's archives and records were analyzed in detail. They showed that Byrd had *not* flown over the North Pole, and despite his claims at the time Byrd knew he had not achieved it. Peary and Cook's claim that each of them had reached the North Pole were also proven to be false.

This meant that Amundsen, Wisting and the crew of the *Norge* were the first to definitely see the North Pole on May 12, 1926.

Amundsen and Wisting were also the first two people in history to be on or above both the North and South Poles. To give you an idea how incredibly difficult it was to be the first to stand at the North Pole, the first team to achieve that was a Soviet Union expedition. They used the Amundsen-Ellsworth method of flying over the Arctic, landing nearby, and then walking to the North Pole in 1948. A US nuclear submarine reached the North Pole under the ice in 1959, and a team of Americans led by Ralph Plaisted, used snow scooters to successfully reach it in 1968. However, the honor of being the first person to journey to the North Pole by dog sledge, the way the early explorers like Nansen and Johansen, Peary and Henson, and Dr. Cook tried to do, and Amundsen would have liked to have done, was Wally Herbert in 1969—the same year men first landed on the moon!

Amundsen deserves international recognition as having achieved: The first to sail the Northwest Passage, the first to reach the South Pole and the first to see the North Pole.

Referring to our original list of eleven projects, described in the introductory chapter of this book, Amundsen was involved in not just two big projects (the Northwest Passage and the South Pole) but in a *third*: the history of flight and the risks and dangers associated with the birth of aviation.

Latter Year Accomplishments—Enduring Legacies

Ocean liners, cargo ships, yachts and even the simple outboard motorboat owe their design to the pioneering work Brunel did on propeller-driven engines. His *Great Eastern* was so enormous that it remained the largest ship ever built for forty-one years. Double hulls, watertight bulkheads, efficient screw-propellers and iron ship design all owe their design to Brunel's legacy.

Roosevelt's River of Doubt expedition explored an important tributary of the Amazon River. His expedition added valuable geographical information to what was already known about the region.

Amundsen's flights took place in the early days of aviation. He showed how flying could complement or supplement other polar expedition journeys. His early polar flights were the precursor to the polar aviation conducted today to assess ice conditions, wildlife habitats and climate change impact.

Brunel, Roosevelt and Amundsen were much more than an engineer, a statesman and an explorer. As discussed in the next chapter, they were quite literally movers and shapers in the geography of our planet.

Chapter 23

Movers and Shapers Of The Earth's Geography

Throughout the span of human existence—300,000 years or longer—humans have been either restricted by the geographical constraints of our locale or forced to use our ingenuity to reshape it to better fit our needs and desires. If human society has two great drives, one is to explore undiscovered places, and the other is to transform (through engineering and political action) those places to service our personal and societal needs better.

Looking back at the long history of human achievement, we have seen specific periods during which society has been propelled forward in big ways thanks to visionary people and technological advancements. One of the most significant developmental times occurred during the Brunel-Roosevelt-Amundsen era spanning from 1825, when the Thames Tunnel was started, to 1914 when the Panama Canal was completed. This era marked the beginning of when humans could make the world a seemingly smaller, and more interconnected, place through better communications and travel.

This period of great achievement catapulted us away from a world reliant on animals, to a world more like the one we live in today. It was during this time that dependence on horse-drawn transport began to wane, and whale oil would no longer be used in lamps.

Pre-1825, the industrial revolution was heavily under way. This new era grabbed all that it had to offer and accelerated its progress.

A good example of this is how fast communication methods advanced. Close to the start of this era the first commercial electric telegraph wire in the world was installed. Thanks to Brunel's foresight it ran along his Wharncliffe Viaduct, built for the Great Western Railway. Partway through the era the *Great Eastern* was built, large enough to hold the entire length of the first transatlantic telegraph cable. This enabled near-instant communication between continents via Morse code and became the precursor to the wire-based communications that dominated the twentieth century. From there we moved to wireless methods.

These endeavors had to start somewhere of course, but they could only have come from the imaginations of the visionaries of that time, who both dreamed them *and* risked their lives, reputations and bank accounts to make them happen.

By 1914—the end of this era—people were able to look at a globe and see an exact representation of the entire planet, all because Amundsen and others had set foot on almost every inch of it. Others like Roosevelt had the wherewithal to reshape even the harshest landscapes, as proven by the building of the Panama Canal.

The great mysteries that began as early as the 1500s—such as the search for the Northwest Passage, or a Latin American waterway linking the great oceans, or ships capable of regularly scheduled transport between the old world of Europe to the new world of America, or how to travel faster than a horse, or whether there was land or sea at the top and bottom of the Earth— these were, by the early 20th Century, all discovered, created or built.

Game-changers

Brunel, Roosevelt and Amundsen spent their lives trying to solve geographical problems that interfered with their vision of how things could be. Perhaps none of them would have thought of their work in this way, but all of them understood that the Earth's geography, in its immense complexity, was nothing more than a series of obstacles to be overcome. The continents with their rocky interiors and river canyons, and the oceans with stormy and ice-choked seas were mere barriers to the most fundamental of human needs: better movement, improved trade, and faster communication.

All that such transformations would require was some intellectual problem solving, organizational acuity, and money coupled with a tremendous amount of self-belief and a never-give-up mindset. The great network of railroads and highways, and the bridges and tunnels along their straight and efficient routes, did not exist in Brunel's day. It is difficult to imagine his world that preceded all these great public works. Horse and carriage was the standard inter-urban transit of the day, trundling along country lanes and over primitive bridges that might have been based upon old Roman road designs, taking days rather than hours to get from place to place.

All that was about to change.

Brunel's successful completion of the Thames Tunnel helped to solve the problem of better commercial exchange between two halves of a London divided by a river. His self-belief and ingenious designs led him to win the contract to build the Great Western Railway, and in turn required him to imagine the most efficient overland route between two large cities, and overcome every obstacle of river and hill between them. Bridges and tunnels were merely engineering problems, each larger and more daring than the last, and demanded newer materials and better techniques to achieve them.

Once Brunel cleared the way travel and trade boomed; commerce doubled and doubled again and continues to grow today. The success of the Great Western Railway sparked similar initiatives not only in England but in the rest of Europe, the Americas and the world. Taken individually the subterranean river tunnel and the railway were of huge importance. But the combination of the two—trains running through tunnels—continues to have a monumental and lasting impact on our modern society.

Brunel's work also led to a growth in international and intercontinental trade which created a demand for new types of ships—ever larger steam-powered iron and then steel ships to replace the smaller sailing vessels of the day. Brunel designed and built the first of these, and later envisioned a ship so large it could carry enough coal to steam around the globe without stopping, while its cavernous holds were stuffed with goods destined for the great ports of the world. His ship, the *Great Eastern*, larger than any ship that had come before, pioneered the start of a global commerce industry which we still depend upon today.

Likewise, Theodore Roosevelt had an innate understanding of the scope and breadth of the United States not just as a nation, but as a vast swath of geography within the scope of the planet. Not just countless square miles of empty land but a broad reach of magnificent rivers and canyons, mountains and plains, deserts and forests. All these could provide the room for a growing population to expand, as well as offer respite from cities and urban life.

Roosevelt understood that the empty spaces were just as important as the urban areas, and would need protection from the rampant developers of his era. In 1901, his rise to the presidency gave him the power to act on this vision and initiate the legislation that would lead to the growth of the National Park system within the United States. This provided a framework for similar conservation efforts to follow throughout the world.

Roosevelt had another vision as well: a view of the world as a web of sea lanes capable of connecting all the ports of the world. Central to this idea was the construction of a canal through the Isthmus of Panama which shortened hazardous seafaring trips by thousands of miles and many months. The canal was not his original idea—the quest dated back to the 1500s—but he was the person to get it done. All it needed was someone with a clear vision who could see that geographical obstacles were just challenges requiring political action and engineering solutions. The Panama Canal opened for trade in 1914, and changed global commerce forever.

Amundsen also saw the world as a whole, grasping at the idea of sea routes linking Europe and Asia, not to the south of the Americas or through them, but above them. Such sea routes through the frozen, long-sought Northwest Passage were less likely to be economically feasible, but the opportunity could not be ignored. Explorers and sea captains thought it could be done. Many had tried, and all had failed.

Until Amundsen.

His *Gjoa* expedition provided a baseline for future geographic discovery: the combination of leadership talents, the right ship, a small multi-skilled crew, and well-defined goals were the key to success.

There remained one more geographical goal, this one also without immediate commercial value. Amundsen was the first to trek overland to the South Pole, the coldest and remotest place on Earth. Here again he proved that some projects are best done by small teams operating with only a small budget. To achieve what he did took a global vision, an intense desire to achieve his goal and a willingness to learn from others, then to lead from the front.

Leaders in an age of achievement

These three titans in their fields shared similar traits. They each saw obstacles that limited how the world functioned. The solutions to overcome them were there waiting to be found by anyone with the vision, ambition and skill to seek them out.

But their stories do not end here. There is one more revelation to come, derived from our years of thinking and writing about these projects and these individuals, and the era in which they lived and worked.

Chapter 24

The Greatest Lesson Of All

There is an even greater lesson we can derive from Brunel, Roosevelt and Amundsen:

Look at every challenge from an engineering, political *and* explorer's point of view, all at the same time.

When we started on this journey, we thought of Brunel as the engineer, Roosevelt as the statesman and Amundsen as the explorer. However, they were much more than their strictly defined titles. Why they emerged as leaders in the "age of achievement" above so many possible competitors is that they each thought like an engineer *and* a statesman *and* an explorer, all the time.

Here are some examples.

Brunel may have been an engineer, but he *explored* the countryside to find the most level route for the Great Western Railway. He didn't leave the job to someone else. He did it himself. He resolved the *political* challenges facing his decision not to route the train through Windsor, home of the royal family's Windsor Castle. He testified for eleven days at Parliament, defending the political value of the railway, and he understood the political gain holding a banquet in the Thames Tunnel would attract.

Roosevelt emerged from his presidency as a statesman. In his early life he threw off the cloaks of his rich, pampered upbringing to *explore* the Western United States as a cowboy. His detailed knowledge and experience of the rivers, valleys, mountains and canyons of the US west enabled him to understand the region, which helped him develop the plans to protect vast swathes of it for national parks and national forests. Clearly skilled in the political arena he also brought his toughness as a cowboy and Rough Rider to debates. When it came to the canal, he understood and appreciated the complexities of the *engineering* challenges once Stevens explained them to him, as well as the engineering required to rid the Canal Zone of yellow fever.

Amundsen was an explorer, yet he was constantly looking at the *engineering* of ships, equipment, clothing, tents, sledges and goggles to prevent snow blindness, all in an effort to find the best solutions. He also knew the *political* landscape of the exploration world. He understood that getting the great Norwegian explorer Fridtjof Nansen to back his plans could lead to introductions to Norwegian benefactors and the royal family—all of whom could sponsor and promote his expeditions.

This is not just a lesson for explorers, engineers and statespeople. It is a lesson for all of us. The challenges we face in our modern lives can become clearer when we adopt the perspective of an explorer, engineer, and a statesperson.

Problems do not exist in a vacuum, and solutions often require a multidisciplinary approach. What the Brunel-Roosevelt-Amundsen decision making approach shows is how those disciplines can be used together.

This approach can be applied to opportunities and challenges both at a personal and career level as well as to national and international issues such as reducing climate change, vaccinating people against pandemics, creating enough food to feed the world's growing population, managing scarce freshwater resources, eliminating plastic in the oceans, and limiting the damage caused by natural disasters.

Not only did these three pioneers set bold goals and achieve remarkable results with their own endeavors, combined they left us with strategies enabling current and future generations to solve the biggest challenges we will collectively encounter in the years ahead.

And one of them even left behind wisdom that was so inspiring it was encoded into the parachute of the Mars Rover spacecraft. The next (and final) chapter reveals that message.

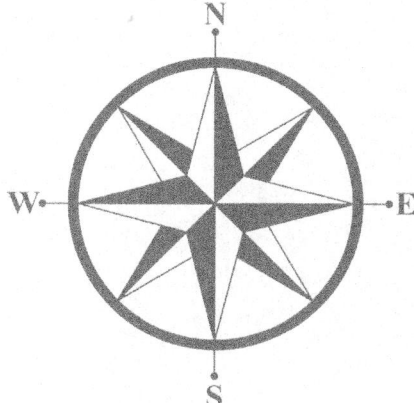

The Mars *Perseverance* rover was aboard this rocket.

Chapter 25
The Ultimate Legacy

Delivered In A Mars Rover Parachute

We started this book by describing how we stumbled upon Brunel, Roosevelt and Amundsen as key figures we wanted to explore further. It was by choosing eleven great achievements that shaped the modern world and our discovery of something *startling, unexpected and exciting* which led us to these three people—who were each instrumental in the success of two or more of those eleven achievements.

A similar thing happened while crafting the ending of this book. We asked, how do we end a book about three visionaries who had such a monumental impact? While pondering this, we stumbled upon something else that was *startling, unexpected and exciting.*

The week we were editing this final chapter, the NASA Rover *Perseverance* touched down successfully on Mars. The landing was broadcast live, and everyone watching around the world saw the large red-and-white patterned parachute open to guide the Rover to the Mars surface. To the ordinary eye, the alternating stripes appeared to be a random, decorative pattern. But it wasn't.

If not decorative, what did it represent?

NASA, a governmental agency devoted to *exploration* and *engineering*, and influenced by *political* willpower and funding, surely wouldn't do something without a dedicated reason and a clear scientific purpose. The NASA engineer describing the landing process told viewers that sometimes NASA embeds a hidden message in its work,[22] where the world (and perhaps in the future, beyond our world) must work to find it. Accepting the challenge, international puzzle enthusiasts tried to decipher it. What had NASA written into the Mars Rover parachute?

It turned out to be a quote, but not just any quote.

Decoded, the three-word quotation was derived from a longer sentence, penned by Theodore Roosevelt and delivered in his stirring "Strenuous Life" speech given in Chicago in April 1899.

"Dare mighty things."

These three inspirational words, delivered to another planet aboard this magnificent triumph of 21st century engineering and interplanetary exploration, were written by a statesman at the end of the 19th century. Roosevelt's larger thought was this:

> "Far better it is to **dare mighty things**, to win glorious triumphs, even though checkered by failure, than to take rank with those poor spirits who neither enjoy much nor suffer much, because they live in the gray twilight that knows not victory nor defeat."

Dare mighty things describes Isambard Kingdom Brunel. It describes Roald Amundsen. And it describes Theodore Roosevelt.

It can also describe you. Perhaps it already does.

Brunel, Amundsen and Roosevelt were human. They were not perfect. But they shared a daring mindset that each of us can emulate. We can set **our own** audacious goals. We can all strive for remarkable results, while accepting that risk, discomfort—and even danger and failure—are just part of the process.

We might achieve our goals, we might not.

But each one of us can be that person who every day gets into the arena (as Roosevelt called it) and dares mighty things.

Appendix

Timeline

This timeline shows the key dates discussed in this book as well as other useful information, to put the people and their achievements in perspective. Items in *italics* provide historical context.

Dates related to:			
Year	BRUNEL	ROOSEVELT	AMUNDSEN
1500s–1700s		*Vasco Núñez de Balboa and others envision a Panama Canal.*	*Sebastian Cabot, Henry Hudson and others fail in their attempts to find the Northwest Passage.*
1799	Richard Dodd fails in attempt to build the first tunnel under the River Thames.		
1806	(Apr) Isambard Kingdom Brunel is born.		
1807–1808	Richard Trevithick fails in attempt to build pilot tunnel under the River Thames.		
1818			*William Parry's first attempt to find the Northwest Passage. He also made attempts in 1819-1820, 1821-1823, and 1824-1825.*
1820			*Antarctica discovered.*
1825	(March) Start of Thames Tunnel construction. Bottle of wine set aside.		
1827	(May) First tunnel flood. (Nov) Banquet in tunnel.		*William Parry expedition to the North Pole, reaching 82° 45' N. A furthest north record.*
1828	(Jan) Second tunnel flood. Six killed. Brunel badly injured. He moves to Clifton, near Bristol, to recover. (Aug) Tunnel bricked up due to lack of funds.		
1831	(Dec) Brunel takes his first train journey and decides he is the one to improve rail travel		
1833	(Mar) Brunel appointed as chief engineer of the Great Western Railway. (Mar–May) Brunel conducts survey to determine best route from London to Bristol.		

Appendix

Year	BRUNEL	ROOSEVELT	AMUNDSEN
1835	(Mar) Thames Tunnel construction restarts after being shut in 1828. (Oct) Brunel identifies London to New York by train and ship as his real aim.	*Panama Canal feasibility study completed by US President Andrew Jackson.*	
1836	(July) Construction starts on SS *Great Western* ship.		
1838	(Mar) SS *Great Western* is launched. (June) Great Western Railway's first trains run from London to Taplow. It is deemed a disaster. (July) Maidenhead Bridge is completed		
1841	(June) Box Tunnel completed, after five years of work. (June) First Great Western Railway train runs from London to Bristol.		
1843	(Mar) Thames Tunnel opens to pedestrian traffic. Bottle of wine set aside in 1825 is finally opened.		
1845	(July) Maiden voyage of SS *Great Britain*.		*John Franklin leaves Britain on his fatal attempt to find the Northwest Passage.*
1854	(Feb) Construction begins on SS *Great Eastern*. (May) London Paddington station opens.		
1855		*Panama Railroad, built by the United States, is completed.*	
1858	(Jan) SS *Great Eastern* launched.	(Oct) Theodore Roosevelt is born.	
1859	(Sept) Isambard Kingdom Brunel dies.		
1864	*(Dec) Clifton Suspension Bridge, which Brunel designed while recuperating from Thames Tunnel flood years before, is completed to commemorate Brunel's great engineering accomplishments.*		

Year	BRUNEL	ROOSEVELT	AMUNDSEN
1865	(Jul) SS Great Eastern *involved in laying the transatlantic cable.* *(Sept) The Thames Tunnel is sold and turned into a train tunnel which is then incorporated into the London Underground network.*		
1872		*(Mar) Yellowstone becomes the first National Park after a law is signed by President Grant.*	(July) Roald Amundsen is born.
1875			*George Nares attempts to reach the North Pole. Achieves 83° 20'N. A new furthest north record.*
1879		*(May) At Paris conference Adolphe Godin de Lépinay explains how to build a lock-based Panama Canal, but is ignored.*	*George De Long attempts to reach the North Pole on the USS* Jeanette. *His ship gets crushed in the ice.*
1881		*French begin building the Panama Canal.*	
1887		Explorer Robert Peary and Matthew Henson seek a viable route through Nicaragua for a canal for the United States. (Dec) Roosevelt helps establish the Boone and Crockett Club, an organization dedicated to fair hunting.	
1888	SS Great Eastern *is sold for scrap*		(May) Amundsen stands on quay in Oslo cheering Nansen's return from a successful crossing of Greenland.
1889		*French abandon their attempt to build the Panama Canal.*	
1890		*(Oct) Sequoia and Yosemite become National Parks. Benjamin Harrison is President.*	
1892	*(May) The Great Western Railway is converted from Brunel's preferred wide-gauge tracks to the British standard narrow gauge.*		
1893			*Fridtjof Nansen's first* Fram *expedition to attempt to reach the North Pole*

Appendix

Year	BRUNEL	ROOSEVELT	AMUNDSEN
1895			*First expedition to land in Antarctica (led by Carsten Borchgrevink).* *Fridtjof Nansen and Hjalmar Johansen leave the Fram to try to reach the North Pole by dog sledge. They achieve 86° 14' N.*
1898		(May–Aug) Roosevelt leads the Rough Riders in the Spanish–American War.	Roald Amundsen is on the *Belgica* Antarctic Expedition (1897–1899).
1900		(Nov) Roosevelt elected as US Vice President.	
1901		(Sept) Theodore Roosevelt becomes youngest US president after McKinley is assassinated. (Nov) Hay-Pauncefote Treaty with Great Britain settles Panama as the ultimate route.	(Mar) Amundsen buys the *Gjoa*. (Summer) Amundsen takes the *Gjoa* on a trial voyage to East Greenland.
1902		(May) Roosevelt establishes Crater Lake as National Park. He goes on to create many National Parks and protect more lands.	
1903		(Nov) Panama Revolution. Roosevelt signs treaty with Panama to create the Panama Canal Zone.	(June) Amundsen's Gjoa Expedition begins its search for the Northwest Passage. (Sept) Amundsen and his men arrive at Gjoahavn.
1904		(Mar) US starts building canal. (May) Roosevelt spends $40 million buying the French infrastructure used in their attempt to build the Panama Canal. (June) John Wallace appointed Chief Engineer of the Panama Canal project. Dr. Gorgas appointed as Chief Sanitary Engineer.	(Apr) Amundsen and Ristvedt start their sledge journey to locate the North Magnetic Pole.
1905		(Jul) Roosevelt appoints John Stevens as Chief Engineer of the Panama Canal project, replacing John Wallace.	(Aug) The *Gjoa* sails out of Gjoahavn.

Year	BRUNEL	ROOSEVELT	AMUNDSEN
1905 cont.		(Dec) Roosevelt funds Dr. Gorgas' mosquito eradication plan.	(Nov-Dec) Amundsen sledges to Eagle, Alaska to announce he has sailed the Northwest Passage. Returns to ship to find that Wiik has died. Due to ice conditions *Gjoa* is forced to overwinter again.
1906		(Feb) Roosevelt accepts Stevens' plan for a lock-based canal. (Oct-Nov) Dr. Gorgas' plan succeeds: last recorded yellow fever death in Canal Zone. (Nov) Roosevelt visits the Panama Canal, becoming the first sitting president to leave the country.	*(Apr) Great San Francisco earthquake* (Oct) The *Gjoa* Expedition arrives in San Francisco. Amundsen is celebrated for having sailed the Northwest Passage.
1907		(Jan–Mar) John Stevens resigns as Chief Engineer of Panama Canal. Replaced by George Washington Goethals.	
1908		(Jan) Roosevelt protects the Grand Canyon by turning it into a National Monument.	
1909		(Mar) Theodore Roosevelt's presidential term ends. He has protected more land than the original thirteen states occupy today. Panama Canal construction continues. Roosevelt and son start a year-long safari in Africa.	*(Summer) Cook and Peary both claim to have reached the North Pole.* (Aug) Amundsen and the *Fram* leave Norway: destination is one of the poles. (Sept) Amundsen telegraphs Scott to inform him that the *Fram* is heading to Antarctica.
1911			(Jan) *Fram* arrives in Antarctica. (Feb) *Fram* and Scott's ship meet unexpectedly in the Bay of Whales. (Oct) Amundsen with a four-man team set out for the South Pole. (Dec) Amundsen and his team arrive at the South Pole, becoming the first to see it and to stand on its location.

Year	BRUNEL	ROOSEVELT	AMUNDSEN
1912		(Oct) Roosevelt shot while campaigning for presidency as part of the Progressive Party.	*(Jan) Captain Robert Scott arrives at the South Pole, five weeks after Amundsen.* *(Mar) Captain Scott and his team perish on their return from the South Pole.* *(Nov) Captain Scott's tent discovered. Amundsen's letter to the King of Norway recovered.*
1913–1914		*(May - Aug 1913) The Culebra Cut at the Panama Canal is completed, and the locks and Cut filled with water.* (Oct 1913 – May 1914) Roosevelt explores the Amazon. *(Aug 1914) World War I starts* (Aug 1914) Panama Canal opens. At that time, it was the most expensive construction project in US history.	
1918-1925			Amundsen embarks on the *Maud* Expedition to drift across the Arctic Ocean in the hope of crossing the North Pole.
1919		(Jan) Theodore Roosevelt dies. *(Feb) Grand Canyon declared a National Park.*	
1925			(May) Amundsen and Ellsworth attempt to fly to the North Pole. They are unsuccessful.
1926			(May) Amundsen, Ellsworth and Nobile fly across the North Pole, three days after Byrd's attempt. This makes them the first to see the North Pole.
1928			(June) Roald Amundsen dies trying to rescue Nobile.
1936			*(May) Fram Museum opens in Oslo*

Year	BRUNEL	ROOSEVELT	AMUNDSEN
1941		(Oct) Theodore Roosevelt is memorialized on Mount Rushmore alongside Presidents Washington, Jefferson and Lincoln. Memorial is built on Native American Land, a controversial decision still to this day.	
1947		(Apr) President Truman establishes the Theodore Roosevelt National Park in North Dakota.	
1958			(Jan) Vivian Fuchs and Edmund Hillary stand at the South Pole and return safely. The first expedition team to do so after Amundsen.
1969			(Apr) Wally Herbert becomes the first to reach the North Pole by dog sledge.
1970	(July) SS Great Britain refloated and brought to the UK.		
1972			(June) Gjoa arrives back in Oslo, having been on display in San Francisco since 1906.
1982	Statue of Brunel erected at London Paddington Station.		
1996			Papers found proving that Byrd did not fly over the North Pole, thus establishing that Amundsen was the first to see the North Pole on his 1926 flight with Ellsworth and Nobile.
1999		Control of the Panama Canal passes from the US to Panama.	
2002	Brunel comes second to Winston Churchill in a public vote for 100 Greatest Britons on a BBC TV show, ranking him higher than Charles Darwin, William Shakespeare and Isaac Newton.		
2010	Brunel Institute founded	Over 1,000,000 ships have passed through the Panama Canal.	
2014–2016		(2016) Panama Canal expansion project completed. Ships 2.5 times larger can now traverse across a new additional waterway.	John Franklin's ships, Erebus and Terror, from his doomed Northwest Passage expedition are discovered in northern Canada.

Appendix | 235

Year	BRUNEL	ROOSEVELT	AMUNDSEN
2017	(Apr) Proven that sunlight streams through Box Tunnel when the sun rises on April 9 (Brunel's birthday).		
2021	Brunel Museum improvements planned.	NASA's Mars Rover lands. A quote from Theodore Roosevelt is embedded in code in its parachute.	
2023-2025			Fram *Museum expansion* planned.

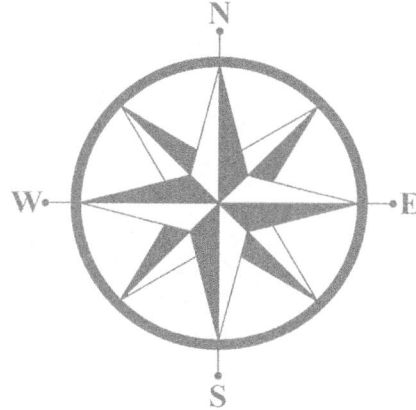

Overlaps of People and Projects

PEOPLE	THE SIX EPIC ENDEAVORS							THEY NEVER STOPPED ACHIEVING		
	Thames Tunnel	Great Western Railway	National Parks	Panama Canal	Northwest Passage	South Pole	Brunel's Ships	River of Doubt	North Pole
Isambard Brunel	X	X					X		
Theodore Roosevelt			X	X		X[1]		X	X[2]
Roald Amundsen			X[3]	X	X	X			X
Richard Trevithick	X	X							
Daniel Gooch		X					X		
Fridtjof Nansen					X	X			X
Robert Peary and Matthew Henson				X		X			X
Oscar Wisting						X			X
Helmer Hanssen					X				X
Richard Byrd						X			X
ACHIEVEMENTS									
Steam power	X	X		X			X		
Railways		X	X	X			X[4]		
Innovations in communications		X					X		
The *Fram* ship						X			X

X[1] Roosevelt sent Amundsen a congratulatory telegram celebrating his achievement of the South Pole.
X[2] Robert Peary sailed to the Arctic in the SS *Roosevelt* to attempt the North Pole.
X[3] Amundsen visited Roosevelt's Maltese Ranch cabin eight years after Roosevelt's death.
X[4] The *Great Western* ship was the seafaring extension of the Great Western Railway

Recomended Reading

Have we whetted your appetite to learn more about the projects and the work of Amundsen, Brunel and Roosevelt? Below is a list of articles, books and documentary films that we have enjoyed and recommend.

A star (✪) has been added to highlight our top book and documentary film recommendations.

Isambard Kingdom Brunel

- ✪ *Brunel: The Man who Built the World*, Steven Brindle (Author), Dan Cruickshank (Introduction), (Weidenfeld & Nicolson, 2006)
- *Brunel and After: The Romance of the Great Western Railway*, Archibold Williams, (Great Western Railway, 1925)
- *Brunel and his World*, John Pudney, (Thames and Hudson, 1974)
- *Brunel in London*, John Christopher (Amberley, 2014)
- ✪ *Isambard Kingdom Brunel*, L.T.C Rolt (Penguin, 1990)
- *Isambard Kingdom Brunel*, John McIlwain (Pitkin, 2019)
- *Isambard Kingdom Brunel*, Richard Tames (Shire, 2009)
- *Isambard Kingdom Brunel: Engineering Knight Errant*, Adrian Vaughan, (John Murray, 1991)
- ✪ *The Brunel's Tunnel*, Andrew Mathewson, Derek Laval, Julia Elton, Eric Kentley, and Robert Hulse (The Brunel Museum, 2006)
- *The Great Brunel*, Chris Morris (Amberley, 2005)
- *The Great Western World Heritage Site, Nomination for Inscription 2010*
- *The Intemperate Engineer—Isambard Kingdom Brunel in His Own Words*, Adrian Vaughan, (Ian Allen, 2010)

Articles
- A History of Track Gauge: How 4 feet, 8½ inches became the standard, (Author) George Hilton, Trains Magazine, May 1, 2006, www.trains.com/trn/train-basics/abcs-of-railroading/a-history-of-track-gauge/
- GWR: A History of the Railways, April 2019, www.gwr.com/destinations-and-events/blogs/2019/april/history-of-the-railways
- History of the Atlantic Cable & Undersea Communications, Great Eastern, (Author) Bill Glover, www.atlantic-cable.com/Cableships/GreatEastern/index.htm
- Railway Wonders of the World: The Story of the GWR, www.railwaywondersoftheworld.com/gwr.html
- Standardising Time: Railways and the Electric Telegraph, Science Museum of London, October 4, 2018, www.sciencemuseum.org.uk/objects-and-stories/standardising-time-railways-and-electric-telegraph
- The Epic Struggle to Tunnel Under the Thames, (Author) Mike Dash, Smithsonian Magazine, Jan 3, 2012, www.smithsonianmag.com/history/the-epic-struggle-to-tunnel-under-the-thames-14638810/
- The First Thames Tunnel, Wonders of the World Engineering Magazine, May 11, 1937, www.wondersofworldengineering.com/thames_tunnel.html
- The Great Eastern Steamship, Scientific American, June 28, 1856, reprinted on Today in Science History, www.todayinsci.com/B/BrunelIsambard/GreatEastern-SciAmJun1856.htm
- The History of Box Tunnel, Network Rail website, www.networkrail.co.uk/who-we-are/our-history/iconic-infrastructure/the-history-of-box-tunnel-wiltshire

Quotations
- The Daniel Gooch quote about Brunel, at the start of Chapter 1, is from the book *Isambard Kingdom Brunel* by Richard Tames, page 43.

Videos
- ◯ *Brunel: The Man who Built Britain*, two-part documentary, Narrator: Rob Bell, (Channel 5 (UK), 2017)
- *Isambard Kingdom Brunel: In Brunel's Tracks from Bristol to Plymouth*, Director: Liam Dale, (KBO Media, 2000)

Theodore Roosevelt

- *America's 26th President: Theodore Roosevelt*, John Gable, National Park Famous American Series, (Eastern National, 2003)
- ◯ *Path between the Seas: The Creation of the Panama Canal 1870–1914*, David McCullough, (Simon & Schuster, 1977)
- *The Autobiography of Theodore Roosevelt*, Theodore Roosevelt (Simon & Brown, 2011)
- *The Building of the Panama Canal in Historical Photographs*, Ulrich Keller, (Dover, 1983)
- *The Naturalist—Theodore Roosevelt, a Lifetime of Exploration, and the Triumph of American Natural History*, Darrin Lunde, (Crown, 2016)
- *The Rise of Theodore Roosevelt*, Edmund Morris, (Modern Library 2001)
- ◯ *The Wilderness Warrior: Theodore Roosevelt and the Crusade for America*, Douglas Brinkley (Harper Collins, 2009)
- *Theodore Rex*, Edmund Morris (Random House, 2002)

Articles

- 10 National Parks in the US you can Reach by Train, (Author) Natalia Lusinski, Lonelyplanet.com, July 7, 2020, www.lonelyplanet.com/articles/us-national-parks-amtrak-train
- NASA Sent a Secret Message to Mars. Meet the People Who Decoded It, (Author) Kenneth Chang, New York Times, Feb 24, 2021, www.nytimes.com/2021/02/24/science/nasa-mars-parachute-code.html
- Teddy, Teddy, Enough Already, (Author) Lewis L. Gould, Oxford University Press OUPBlog, Feb 20, 2012, https://blog.oup.com/2012/02/teddy-theodore-roosevelt/
- The Amazonian Expedition That Nearly Killed Theodore Roosevelt, Evan Andrews, History.com, Sept 4, 2018, www.history.com/news/the-amazonian-expedition-that-nearly-killed-theodore-roosevelt
- The Speech That Saved Teddy Roosevelt's Life, (Author) Patricia O'Toole, Smithsonian, Nov 2012 www.smithsonianmag.com/history/the-speech-that-saved-teddy-roosevelts-life-83479091/
- When Teddy Roosevelt Was Shot in 1912, a Speech May Have Saved His Life, (Author) Christopher Klein, History.com, July 21, 2019 www.history.com/news/shot-in-the-chest-100-years-ago-teddy-roosevelt-kept-on-talking

Quotations

- The Man in the Arena quote at the start of this book and in Chapter 8 is from Theodore Roosevelt's speech, delivered in Paris in April 1910, called "Citizenship in a Republic." The full text is available on www.leadershipnow.com/tr-citizenship.html

- "Death had to take him sleeping …" quote at the start of Chapter 7 is from a cable sent by Thomas Marshall, the Vice President of the United States at the time of Roosevelt's death.
- The "Nothing in this world is worth having or worth doing …" quote at the start of Chapter 11 is from Roosevelt's speech in November 1910, to the Iowa State Teacher's Association called, "American Ideals in Education"
- "Never throughout history has a man who lived a life of ease left a name worth remembering." This insightful quote at the start of Chapter 22 is widely attributed to Theodore Roosevelt, for example on www.brainyquote.com/quotes/theodore_roosevelt_165112

Videos

✪ TR: The Story of Theodore Roosevelt, two-part documentary, PBS, 1996

Roald Amundsen

- *Conquest of the South Pole: Antarctic Exploration 1906–1931*, J. Gordon Hayes (Thornton Butterworth, 1932)
- *Ice Ship Fram: The Epic Voyages of the Polar Adventurer*, Charles Johnson, (ForeEdge, 2014)
- *Lessons from the Arctic: How Roald Amundsen won the Race to the South Pole*, Geir Kløver, (The Fram Museum, 2017)
- *My Life as an Explorer*, Roald Amundsen, (Amberley Publishing, reprinted 2008) originally published in 1927
- *Scott and Amundsen—The Race for the South Pole*, Roland Huntford, (Continuum, 2010)

- *The Arctic Grail—The Quest for the North West Passage and the North Pole*, Pierre Berton, (McClelland and Stewart, 1988)
- *The Amundsen Photographs, Captain Roald Amundsen*, Roland Huntford (editor), (Hodder & Stoughton, 1987)
- *The Great Explorers and their Journeys of Discovery*, Beau Riffenburgh, (Andre Deutsch, 2017)
- ✪ *The Last Viking: The Life of Roald Amundsen*, Conqueror of the South Pole, Stephen Brown, (Aurum Press, 2012)
- *The North Pole*, Robert E. Peary with foreword by Theodore Roosevelt (Hodder and Stoughton, 1910)
- *The Northwest Passage*, Roald Amundsen, (Dutton, 1908)
- *The South Pole: An Account of the Norwegian Antarctic Expedition in the "Fram": 1910–1912*, Roald Amundsen (Indy Publishing, 2002) originally published in 1912
- *The South Pole Expedition 1910-1912: The Roald Amundsen Diaries*, Geir Kløver, editor, (The Fram Museum, 2010)
- *When Your Life Depends on It: Extreme Decision Making Lessons from the Antarctic*, Brad Borkan and David Hirzel, (Terra Nova Press, 2017)

Articles
- Gjoa Monument, San Francisco, Atlas Obscura, www.atlasobscura.com/places/gjoa-monument
- S.F. welcomed 1st Northwest Passage sailor but mistreated sloop, (Author) Gary Kamiya, San Francisco Chronicle, May 8, 2015, www.sfchronicle.com/bayarea/article/S-F-welcomed-1st-Northwest-Passage-sailor-but-6252181.php
- Sebastian Cabot, Newfoundland & Labrador Heritage, www.heritage.nf.ca/articles/exploration/sebastian-cabot.php

- The Gjoa Expedition (1903–1906), Fram—The Polar Exploration Museum website, https://frammuseum.no/polar-history/expeditions/the-gjoa-expedition-1903-1906/
- The Gjoa in Golden Gate Park, OutsideLands.org, www.outsidelands.org/gjoa1.php
- The Legacy of Arctic Explorer Matthew Henson, (Author) James Mills, National Geographic, February 2014, www.nationalgeographic.com/adventure/adventure-blog/2014/02/28/the-legacy-of-arctic-explorer-matthew-henson/
- Who Discovered the North Pole? (Author) Bruce Henderson, Smithsonian Magazine, April 2009, www.smithsonianmag.com/history/who-discovered-the-north-pole-116633746/

Quotations
- "Adventure is just bad planning" is a quote attributed to Amundsen in various publications.
- "Victory awaits him who has everything in order ..." quote at the start of Chapter 5 can be found in many sources including the book, *The Last Viking: The Life of Roald Amundsen, Conqueror of the South Pole*.
- "The secret to my success ..." quote at the start of Chapter 6 is from *The Last Viking: The Life of Roald Amundsen, Conqueror of the South Pole* (page 187)

Videos
- ✪ *Amundsen*, Espen Sandberg (Director), Ravn Lanesskog (Writer), (Espen Horn, 2019)

A note about our research methods

We approach the research for all of our books the old-fashioned way: by reading the leading publications on the subject, visiting museums and speaking with experts. All of the statements in this book have been checked and re-checked against works and articles for historical accuracy using multiple different sources to assess the accuracy of the statement.

We invited historians to review drafts of the book. When we needed certain elements that could be gleaned from the internet, we relied only on a few trusted sites: Brunel Museum, Encyclopedia Britannica, Fram Museum, National Geographic, National Park Service, Panama Canal Museum, Royal Geographical Society, Royal Museums Greenwich, Scott Polar Research Institute, Smithsonian, and even then we double and triple checked with other sources. We used specialist sites for currency, distance and temperature conversions.

The developmental editors who worked with us are experts in historical non-fiction books and have previously edited books related to the topics in this book.

Acknowledgements

When we were formulating the ideas for this book we purposely limited the number of people to a small group who knew the full breadth of what we were working on. These people included: Cathy Cooper (photographer), Seb Coulthard (historian, polar adventurer and lecturer), Stuart Leggett (polar book dealer and historian), Shari Powell (editor) as well as a few close family members.

Thanks to the wonderful and supportive multinational creative team we assembled for our first book, *When Your Life Depends on It*, we were able to call upon the services of the many people who helped us produce that book. The very first person we contacted was the highly talented audiobook narrator, Dennis Kleinman. His narration of *When Your Life Depends on It* led to a Voice Arts Award nomination as a finalist for best audiobook in the history category and a red-carpet appearance for Dennis and Brad Borkan at Warner Bros Studios in Hollywood.

Our developmental editors were Paula Elmore, highly recommended to us by our friend and polar author Michael Smith, and Lisa Fitzpatrick, whose relevant experience included books on Antarctica and the US National Parks. Our copy editor was Kate Gallagher of Nerd Girl Edits. Together they brilliantly transformed our rough manuscript into what it is today. Anne Sharples created the cover and interior of our book.

As part of the research for this book we learned from the Brunel Museum former director Robert Hulse and Brunel Institute director Tim Bryan, lead ranger at the Theodore Roosevelt Birthplace National Historic Site Alyssa Parker Geisman, and the Fram Museum director Geir Kløver.

We received valued corrections from early readers including best-selling author William Myers, Jr, as well as Lisa Chalmers and Dr. Peter Bauer. We are also especially grateful to Karen Carpenter, a UK-based business consultant, who sharpened the decision lessons throughout the book.

The Antarctic community, of which we are both active members, have influenced our thinking not just about Amundsen and polar history, but of all history, and this helped broaden our thinking. This included the Scott Polar Research Institute team: Dr. John Shears, Charlotte Connelly and Celene Pickard; the Shackleton Museum in Athy, Ireland including Frank Taaffe, Seamus Taaffe and Kevin Kenny; the Shackleton Appreciation Facebook group run by Stephen Scott-Fawcett; the Antarctic Circle and South Polesium Conferences run by Robert Stephenson; the Fram Museum run by Geir Kløver and his remarkable team; the South Georgia Association; the James Caird Society; the UK Antarctic Heritage Trust; and the Royal Geographical Society.

Our many friends in the Polar community all influenced our thinking. They included polar historians, Antarctic adventurers, and descendants of the early explorers: Joan Boothe, Bob Burton, Wendy Driver, Sir Ranulph Fiennes, Bob Headland, Don and Val Kerr, Jim and Geraldine McAdam, Baz Gray, Tim Jarvis, Dr. Cathy Corbishley Michel, Geoff Michel, Katie Murray, Joe O'Farrell, Sam Richmond, Falcon Scott, Alexandra Shackleton, Jonathan Shackleton, Judy Skelton, Michael Smith, Anne Strathie, Dr. Isobel Williams, Dr. David Wilson and many others.

Also for research purposes one or both of us traveled to Antarctica, the Brunel Museum and the site of the Thames Tunnel in London, the Falkland Islands (where the mizzen mast of Brunel's *Great Britain* ship is on display). We also visited the Fram Museum, the National Library of Norway and Amundsen's home, all three of which are located in Oslo. In New York, we saw the Roosevelt Birthplace Museum and the American Museum of Natural History in New York City. Other locations visited included South Georgia island and its wonderful polar museum. Each of us have seen many of the great US national parks including Yosemite, the Grand Canyon and Muir Woods National Monument. In the UK, we visited the National Railway Museum in York, the Royal Geographical Society in London, the Scott Polar Research Institute in Cambridge, and have also travelled the length of the Great Western Railway.

For the Antarctic trip, Brad would like to express his deep-felt thanks to Angie Butler who runs the Ice Tracks Travel Agency and her incredible team, Cris Mason and Caro Mantella, and to the crew and staff of the Hebridean Sky ship run by Polar Latitudes.

Additional people who influenced our work included our wonderfully supportive speakers' agent Diana Boulter who runs DBA Speakers, and interviewer-extraordinaire Bonnie D. Graham. The author community has been very supportive. We would like to thank Orna Ross and Debbie Young at the Alliance of Independent Authors, the BytetheBook Author Club, as well as the Society of Authors and the many members of the London Indie Author group.

Our website www.extreme-decisions.com was created by Leah Matthews of Virtual Studio and supported by Jacques Soudan. Ideas for book titles came from Richard Blumberg, Don Fishbein, Michael Grist, Charles Harris, Leena H., Nicola Rossi, Hazel Stix, Katheryne Tollemache and Holly Worton.

Thanks also to our families and close friends who, for the last two years, listened patiently while we regaled them (a few might say too many times) with stories of tunnel floods, railway construction, the size of the Panama Canal locks and the race for the South Pole, all without ever being told what the book was really about until it was nearly ready for publication.

The authors are most deeply indebted to the following people for their unflagging support and encouragement. Brad to his wife, Anne and daughter Brittany, and David to Alice Cochran, the light of his life.

While we gained invaluable insights from all the organizations and people involved in this book, any errors are our own.

Notes about the Photographs

Back cover: Roald Amundsen: In furs for a studio photograph in June 1899. Image courtesy of the National Library of Norway, Image: bldsa_NBRA0005.

Isambard Kingdom Brunel: In front of the roll of chains designed for the launch of the Great Eastern in 1857. Image was provided by the Institution of Civil Engineers.

Theodore Roosevelt: Presidential photograph taken in May 1904. Image courtesy of the United States Library of Congress, Prints & Photographs Division, Image: LC-ppmsca-04598.

Part 1: Brunel standing in front of the roll of chains designed for the launch of the Great Eastern in 1857. Image was provided by the Institution of Civil Engineers.

Chapter 1: The Thames Tunnel as it appeared when it was first opened, from the book. Antique print taken from the book, *Old and New London: A Narrative of its History, its People, and its Places*, by Walter Thornbury, 1876

Chapter 4: London Paddington Station. Photo by Cathy Cooper.

Part 2: Theodore Roosevelt: Presidential photograph taken in May 1904. Image courtesy of the United States Library of Congress, Prints & Photographs Division, Image: LC-ppmsca-04598.

Chapter 8: Arches National Park. Photo by Ron Borkan.

Chapter 11: Panama Canal. Photo by Dave Heidtke.

Part 3: Roald Amundsen: Posing in furs for a studio photograph in June 1899. Image courtesy of the National Library of Norway, Image: bldsa_NBRA0005.

Chapter 15: Sea ice. Photo by Brad Borkan.

Chapter 18: Antarctica. Photo by Brad Borkan.

Part 4: Earth: Image taken by a NASA satellite. https://images.nasa.gov/details-0202795

Chapter 25: NASA rocket carrying the Mars Perseverance rover lifting off. Image taken by NASA. https://images.nasa.gov/details-KSC-20200730-PH-AWG03_0017

About the Authors

Brad Borkan has had an interest in how people survive and thrive in almost impossible situations for as long as he can remember. He is an author and lecturer and has presented at business and Antarctic conferences, appeared on cable TV in the US, and has been a guest on podcasts and internet radio interview programs. His talks focus on leadership, teamwork and winning against the odds.

Brad has traveled to all seven continents. On a 114-strong passenger "expedition" cruise to Antarctica, he gave a guest lecture about the first book he co-authored with David Hirzel, *When Your Life Depends on It: Extreme Decision Making Lessons from the Antarctic*. Originally from the US and now based in London, Brad was honored to be made a Fellow of the Royal Geographical Society. He is also a member of the Society of Authors and sits on the Committee of the Friends of the Scott Polar Research Institute.

David Hirzel is a maritime historian, author and small business owner. His enduring interest in world history and the evolution of societies focuses on the study of polar exploration, and his vocation in architecture expands those interests. He has applied his knowledge to this book through his exploration of the history of modern engineering from Brunel's pioneering work in transportation technology to the monumental systems of the Panama Canal, to the triumphs of Amundsen's discoveries.

David works out of his design office overlooking the sea in Pacifica, CA, with a drafting table, a wide desk and an even wider library of technical and history books to hand. His polar books include a three-part polar biography of the Irish explorer Tom Crean who was a key player in Captain Scott and Ernest Shackleton's expeditions. David is also a popular cruise ship lecturer on polar and maritime exploration.

A note to our readers:

Audacious Goals, Remarkable Results is the second book in our Borkan-Hirzel series on decision making. Our books draw on the experiences of heroes from the past to teach us how to make better decisions at a personal and business level.

We are currently working on several additional books.
We love hearing from readers and can be contacted via our website: www.extreme-decisions.com. Please join our mailing list. Sign-up details are on our website.

If you enjoyed this book, we would be most grateful for a review on Amazon, Goodreads or any other sites that readers might visit. Thank you in advance for doing this. It means a lot to us.
The opening chapter of our first co-authored book, *When Your Life Depends on It: Extreme Decision Making Lessons from the Antarctic*, appears on the next pages.

Endnotes

1 Reference in the book, The Brunels' Tunnel, page 46.

2 For comparison purposes, the fastest manned space rocket can travel at almost 25,000 mph (40,000 km/h) and the fastest train, the Shanghai Maglev, can travel at 267 mph (430 km/h).

3 Based on the *Webster Dictionary* definition in the 1820s.

4 From Brunel's diary, written in December 1835.

5 "Light at the end of the tunnel: sun shines for Brunel's birthday," *The Guardian* newspaper, April 10, 2017, article by Steven Morris. www.theguardian.com/technology/2017/apr/10/isambard-kingdom-brunel-birthday-box-tunnel-bath-sun

6 The British government decided to withdraw the World Heritage Site application because they understood that the committee's desire was to give the designation to more sites from less prominent countries.

7 www.history.com/news/shot-in-the-chest-100-years-ago-teddy-roosevelt-kept-on-talking

8 Julian Street published a book in 1915 titled, *The Most Interesting American*. When asked about this, Julian Street replied, "Well, if he isn't, who is?" Reference: *America's 26th President: Theodore Roosevelt*, National Park Famous American Series, pages 2–3.

9 The Man in the Arena quote is from Theodore Roosevelt's speech, delivered in Paris in April 1910, called "Citizenship in a Republic." The full text is available on www.leadershipnow.com/tr-citizenship.html

10 The spelling of Assuan in Roosevelt's essay is the spelling of that era. Today, the name of the region is written as Aswan.

11 National Park Service: www.nps.gov/thro/learn/historyculture/theodore-roosevelt-quotes.htm

12 Isambard Kingdom Brunel was educated in France.

13 If that same calculation was done in 1999 (since the majority of very tall buildings were built after the year 2000), one lock stood on its end would have become the tenth tallest building in America.

14 Ship movements were measured using the original channel for the Panama Canal. A second, wider channel was added to the canal in 2016.

15 This statement underestimates the amount of dirt dug out to build the Panama Canal. Not only could the amount of earth removed build the equivalent of the Great Wall of China from Newfoundland, Canada to the

Florida Keys, but there would be enough dirt left over to continue the wall back up the US east coast, past Washington DC.

16 Amundsen's first meeting with Georg von Neumayer is described in Amundsen's autobiography, *My Life as an Explorer: A Memoir*.

17 *The North Pole*, by Robert E. Peary, 1910. Introduction written by Theodore Roosevelt, page iv.

18 In engineering, a factor of safety expresses how much stronger a system is than it needs to be for an intended use. That Brunel's structures and the locks of Roosevelt's Panama Canal are still in use today—all of them over 100 years old—is testament to the concept. Make it once, far sturdier than you really think it ought to be, and it will surely last.

19 A copy of the telegram was kindly provided to the authors by Geir Kløver, Director of the Fram Museum.

20 Between the time of Brunel's initial thoughts about the *Great Eastern* and when it was launched in 1858, a few ships like the *Persia*, that were somewhat larger than Brunel's *Great Britain*, had been launched. The *Great Eastern* exceeded the dimensions of all those ships by the dimensions stated.

21 Photograph of Amundsen in front of Roosevelt's Maltese Cross cabin: www.digitalhorizonsonline.org/digital/collection/uw-ndshs/id/14097/

22 Details about the parachute can be found in a New York Times article titled, *NASA Sent a Secret Message to Mars. Meet the People Who Decoded It*, (Author) Kenneth Chang, Feb 24, 2021. The press conference where NASA engineer Allen Chen explained that there was a coded message in the Mars Rover parachute can be watched on YouTube: https://www.youtube.com/watch?v=Rp4E4h-h1JM

Brad Borkan and David Hirzel are co-authors of: *When Your Life Depends on It: Extreme Decision Making Lessons from the Antarctic.*

Awards
- 1st Place: Chanticleer International Book Awards for Insightful Non-fiction
- Finalist: Wishing Shelf Book Awards for Non-fiction
- Finalist: Voice Arts Awards: Best Audiobook—History category.

Endorsements

"A remarkable book"
Sir Ranulph Fiennes, world's greatest living polar explorer

"Polar book of the year"
Jonathan Shackleton, Antarctic historian

Opening Chapter from
"When Your Life Depends on It:
Extreme Decision Making Lessons from the Antarctic"

It's Your Call

Antarctica—the early 1900's.
The only communication is as far as you can shout.

You and your two companions are nearing the end of a fifteen-hundred-mile trek to a nameless spot on the South Polar Plateau.

To say conditions are harsh would be an understatement. Temperatures can get so low that you risk frostbite even when bundled in your reindeer-hide sleeping bags. The jagged, frozen landscape provides constant challenges, including the danger of crevasses cracking open unexpectedly beneath your feet, plunging you into their depths. At times you have been on the verge of starvation.

Your presence here today is the result of countless decisions great and small made along the way. Right now you are faced with a decision greater than any that came before. One of your companions has fallen so ill with scurvy he can no longer walk.

Seventy miles of dangerous terrain lie ahead before you reach the safety of your base camp, and you will have to drag him on the sledge, adding an almost unbearable weight to that of your ice-encrusted tent and the last remnants of food keeping you alive.

The reality of the situation is grim. You must maintain a steady pace each day, regardless of the weather, to reach the next depot of supplies before those on hand run out. Your daily distances have fallen off, and continue to fall. The sick man, already perilously near death, is unlikely to survive the remainder of the journey.

With his extra weight further reducing your daily mileage, neither will you and your other companion. You all know the fate that lies ahead. The sick man tells the two of you to leave him here on the Barrier and march on ahead with the sledge and supplies, to save yourselves while you can. The three of you have developed a close camaraderie during your long walk; leaving him to perish on the ice is inconceivable. The obvious, ethical, human decision: to shoulder your burden and do your best.

The situation is not so straightforward. You are seamen and the sick man is your commanding officer. He has commanded you to leave him behind. The one thing that has been repeatedly drilled into you throughout your entire working life is this: there is no occasion on which you can refuse to comply with the order of an officer.

To obey means the two of you have at least a chance at survival; to refuse is mutiny, and certain death for all three of you.

The choice is now yours—it's your call. How will you decide?

This was a real event faced by real people. They did have to make this call. Their decision and the outcome may surprise you ...

You will find the rest of the story in *When Your Life Depends on It: Extreme Decision Making Lessons from the Antarctic* by Brad Borkan and David Hirzel. It is available on Amazon and other online booksellers. The audiobook is available on Audible and iTunes.

Printed in Great Britain
by Amazon